FROM WARRIORS
TO SOLDIERS

FROM WARRIORS TO SOLDIERS

A History of American Indian Service in the United States Military

GARY ROBINSON & PHIL LUCAS

iUniverse, Inc.
New York Bloomington

From Warriors to Soldiers
A History of American Indian Service in the United States Military

Copyright © 2010 by Gary Robinson

iUniverse Star
an iUniverse, Inc. imprint

iUniverse books may be ordered through booksellers or by contacting:

iUniverse
1663 Liberty Drive
Bloomington, IN 47403
www.iuniverse.com
1-800-Authors (1-800-288-4677)

ISBN: 978-1-936236-00-8 (pbk)
ISBN: 978-1-936236-01-5 (ebk)

Library of Congress Control Number: 978193623600

Printed in the United States of America

iUniverse rev. date: 1/26/2010

Publication of this book was made possible in part
through the financial support of the *United Indians
of All Tribes Foundation*, Seattle, Washington.
For more information, go to www.unitedindians.org.

To my father, Don Robinson,
a veteran of World War II and the finest
role model any son could have.

Gary Robinson

Contents

Dear Readers, Friends, and Relatives,

On behalf of United Indians of All Tribes Foundation (UIATF), I would like to extend our great appreciation and heartfelt thanksgiving to our very dear brother, the late Phil Lucas, and to Gary Robinson for all the great love, energy, dedication, sensitivity, and caring they displayed in the creation of *From Warriors to Soldiers*, which poignantly reflects the voices and dedicated service of our Native American warriors and soldiers.

UIATF was honored to contribute funding to support the publication of this long-overdue book, and we look forward to continuing our support by developing a complementary Web site that will provide an opportunity for our warriors, veterans, and their friends and relatives to relate the heartfelt stories of military service and sacrifice reflected in *From Warriors to Soldiers*.

As always, it is our prayer that you and your beloved ones are in the very best of health and happiness.

With warm, respectful, and loving greetings,

Phil Lane Jr.
Chief Executive Officer
United Indians of All Tribes Foundation
Seattle, Washington

Acknowledgments

The information for this book was intensively and laboriously researched, first in the 1990s, with the intention of producing a documentary television series for national broadcast. Native American Public Telecommunications provided initial funding to conduct the research and prepare the scripts, for which I am grateful.

However, when it came time to raise the several hundred thousand dollars required to produce the series, no funding agencies were interested. Phil and I spent many years attempting to procure financing, and the project went through several permutations in an effort to provide the proposal format required by various funding sources.

It wasn't until my very dear friend and partner of twenty-five years, Phil Lucas, passed away in early 2007 that the idea of converting all the material into book form came into being. Phil was a Choctaw filmmaker and teacher who dedicated his life to telling true stories about Native Americans through films and television documentaries. His gentle, intuitive spirit guided us through many special and rewarding experiences within the largely misunderstood and misinterpreted worlds of native peoples.

I miss him and will be indebted to him for the rest of my life.

As a team, Phil and I researched, wrote, and co-produced many award-winning television and video projects over the years concerning Native American peoples, cultures, and contemporary topics. We became expertly familiar with research sources and techniques and developed our own "native" style of documentary and educational filmmaking.

I also want to acknowledge the financial support provided by the United Indians of All Tribes Foundation, headquartered in Seattle. This organization has worked tirelessly for more than thirty years to improve the quality of life for native peoples in the Northwest. Its contribution has literally made this publication possible.

Introduction

"What does it mean to be a warrior in the traditional Native American cultural sense? It means doing what's right, even when it's difficult and requires sacrifice."

—Native American Vietnam War Veteran

There's an American military cemetery and memorial in France that few Americans are aware of. It is located twenty-six miles north of Verdun at a place called Meuse-Argonne, and it contains the remains of more than fourteen thousand American military personnel. There you will find row upon row of identical gravestones bearing the name of American soldiers killed during World War I. You might be surprised to read the names on some of the gravestones. Mixed in with the "typical" GI Joe names are those of Native Americans, names like "Joe Standing Bear" and "Leon Little Wolf." These men, these Native American soldiers, most of them volunteers, lie here—so far from the sacred land of their fathers.

Some seventeen thousand American Indians volunteered for military service during World War I, even though they weren't allowed to become citizens of the United States until 1924, seven years after that war ended.

The truth is that from the American Revolution up until today, Native American people have served the United States unfailingly in battle and have sacrificed their lives and resources for a nation that was once their enemy. Today, Native American men and women continue to enlist and serve with distinction in all branches of the armed services at rates that far exceed other ethnic groups, and their tribal communities carry on proud traditions that include the honoring of those who've participated in the defense of their homeland.

This book tells the untold story of those brave heroes, and it is written in honor of all Native American veterans of all tribes to bring much-deserved attention to the dedication and sacrifice offered up by Native Americans of all tribes in all parts of the United States.

Gary Robinson
Santa Ynez, CA

PART ONE

Native Warriors: Myth and Reality

The Warrior—*The Chiricahua Apache who became known as Geronimo was the epitome of the Indian warrior. Though originally a peaceful farmer and family man, he led the resistance against white encroachment of Indian lands after his family was killed by U.S. soldiers. (National Archives Photo)*

A True Warrior—*Typical of most tribal leaders, Nez Perce Chief Joseph avoided warfare whenever possible. However, when the United States took his tribal lands, he led his people on a cross-country retreat that managed to elude the army's best military commanders beyond all expectations. His maneuvers were studied and later taught to cadets at West Point. (National Archives Photo)*

PART ONE—NATIVE WARRIORS: MYTH AND REALITY

Native American powwows—you can find dozens of these colorful, social events during spring and summer months in major cities or on any of the three hundred or so Indian reservations in the United States. Based on ancient Plains Indian traditions, modern powwows began springing up around the United States after World War II as a way for the growing urban Indian populations to maintain cultural connections within what was to them an alien environment.

A powwow is a bountiful blend of tribal singing, dancing, eating, camping, and visiting among family and friends that attracts dancers, drummers, vendors, indigenous craftspeople, and spectators from far and wide. They all come for one reason: to participate in something uniquely Native American, something that preserves and honors the best aspects of native cultures.

Dancers often compete for prize money in a variety of native dance categories, including the Jingle Dress, Ladies Buckskin, Men's Traditional, and Men's Fancy Dance, to name a few. Each dance category is known for its own style of movement and regalia, while each dancer within a category expresses his or her own individuality through variations in dance style and clothing.

Every dance session of a powwow begins with the Grand Entry, the procession that brings all the dancers into the arena. At the front of the line, moving to the beat of the drum and bringing in the American flag, state flag, and traditional Eagle Staff, are Native American veterans. They may be dressed in dance regalia, street clothes, or sometimes their military uniforms, proudly carrying the colors and leading all the dancers into the arena.

And the crowds of onlookers stand, doff their hats, and watch attentively as the flags and the veterans circle the arena. To many, this is more than pomp and circumstance; it is part of a sacred culture. It is one of the more public ways that native people honor their veterans and acknowledge their sacrifice and service for the good of the nation.

Why have American Indians served, and why do they continue to serve, a government that has betrayed and broken promises to native peoples for multiple generations? Why do so many American Indians take pride in military service?

Native American men and women who have served their country's military with pride may be able to help answer such questions. They often gather to share experiences and insights during powwow weekends, as a dozen or so did at a 4th of July powwow a few years ago. They begin by talking about the reasons for Native American service.

The Powwow: A place of honor
for Native American veterans

At Native American powwows, it is traditional for veterans to be honored for their sacrifice and service by bringing in the colors during the Grand Entry, which begins each session of dancing. Photo taken by the author at the Oneida Powwow, July, 1992.

Among the flags carried by the veterans is the tribe's Eagle Staff, featuring a row of eagle feathers, each feather representing a tribal member who has served. Photo by the author.

Menomenee Vietnam Veteran Apesanahkwat proudly displays his military service in this unique display of quill work on his powwow dance regalia. Photos taken circa 1992.

"Most American Indians don't view their military service as something simply patriotic," stated Northern Cheyenne Vietnam veteran Windy Shoulderblade. "It's something deeper than that, passed down from generation to generation. It was our fathers—it was our grandfathers. The warrior status was always an achievement for Indian men. They have always gone to face the enemy when it was their turn."

"Members of my tribe, the Oneida, have served the United States in every conflict since the Revolutionary War," Amos Christjohn offered. "We helped out General Washington back then and taught the American colonials how to fight the Indian way."

"Native Americans have a great deal of respect for the Supreme Being, the Creator," stated Douglas Long, a Korean vet of the Winnebago tribe. "The eagle is the one who can fly the highest, and the elders have taught us to respect this bird. We hold the eagle feather to be very sacred. Each one of the tribes has an Eagle Staff, and the only way that another feather can be added to that staff is through experiences of defending their territory. And so that tradition continues even today."

The reasons for Native American participation in the U.S. military are as complex and unique as their ways of fighting. Historically, the unique style of native warfare was noticed by British American colonists and military personnel in the 1700s.

"Indians are the only match for Indians, and without them [on our side] we shall ever fight on unequal terms," stated then Colonel George Washington in 1756 during the French and Indian War, an extended war fought between the British and the French from 1754 to 1763.[1] Caught in the middle of an essentially European-based war, American Indians fought on both sides of that conflict.

British General John Forbes, writing of his experiences during the same war, attested to the natives' prowess at what would come to be called "guerilla warfare tactics," a term coined many generations later. In a letter from the battlefield to his superiors in Philadelphia, he told of the "howling out in the forest" that came from Native American warriors who flitted from one tree trunk to another. Forbes watched in horror as British soldier after British soldier fell to snipers' bullets, though the sources for the mortal rounds could not be located.

General George Washington remembered well his previous first-hand experiences with the effectiveness of Indian warriors, and after the Revolutionary War got under way, he convinced the Continental Congress to allow him to employ Indians in his colonial army. He knew they'd be of excellent use mixed with his regular army as scout and light troops.

Oneida veteran Amos Christjohn offered additional insights regarding native warfare techniques. "We learned a lot about conducting warfare from watching our four-legged brothers, the animals, and we have always respected the strength of their powers," he said.

Differentiating between Euro-American warfare tactics and Native American techniques, Windy shared something he learned from his tribe. "The Cheyenne rule was for each member of a warrior band not to wait for orders or try to do like the rest," Windy explained. "He could retreat if he wanted to, but he would be criticized by many who watched the battle. White Elk and the others used to say the white men have a poor way of fighting. They all listen to one man say 'shoot,' and sometimes the warriors could come up behind them before they had time to turn around."

Anthropologist and author Jack Weatherford has studied and written about the accomplishments of Native Americans, including American Indian warfare techniques. His book *Native Roots* includes a chapter on this topic.

According to Weatherford, Indians did not line up in formation and march onto a large field, as did European armies. They fought the same way they hunted, using stealth, camouflage, and familiarity with the forest to their advantage. Indians also used traps, lures, decoys, and calls effectively in warfare, as in hunting. As noted earlier, the American colonists learned how valuable this kind of fighting was long before the Revolution and began adopting these techniques, as well.[2]

During the 1700s and 1800s, the accepted view among Americans and Europeans was that Native Americans were inferior, war-loving savages.

As will be discussed later, early explorers purposefully created and disseminated this image of Indians to justify the wholesale displacement and genocide of indigenous peoples. This myth, however, experienced some revisionism after the Second World War, due in part to the well-publicized heroism of Indian soldiers in both the Pacific and European war theaters. For some unknown reason, President Harry Truman took a particular interest in Indian affairs and Indian leaders.

His thoughts on the subject are found in the papers kept in the Harry S. Truman Library.

They weren't an inferior race at all, of course. They were wonderfully wise people, and there were Indian setups that were almost ideal systems of government, almost parallel with the government of the United States under the Constitution. The Indians had some very great leaders of the Indian tribes, men like Pontiac in Michigan, Tecumseh of the Shawnee, Geronimo down in the Southwest, Black Kettle of the Cheyenne, Sitting Bull and Crazy Horse of the Sioux and Chief Joseph of the Nez Perce, who performed one of the greatest military maneuvers in the history of the world.

He took his whole tribe—something like eight hundred men, women and children—and outmaneuvered practically the whole cavalry of the United States, including one of the great strategists of the Civil War, General Howard, moving his people over a thousand miles up toward Canada—a record that has never been equaled. Howard's outfit and another force of soldiers were miles apart, and neither general knew where the other was, but Chief Joseph knew where both of them were and he got his people out. Finally, after the cavalry kept chasing him and killed off many of his people, he surrendered, but old Joseph out-marched them all—they never did catch up with him, not really.[3]

It is ironic that Chief Joseph was not actually a "War Chief" at all. Like Sitting Bull of the Lakota and Apache leader Geronimo, Joseph was the spiritual leader of his tribal nation who rose to the occasion of fighting to save the lives of his people.

According to Dee Brown in his respected history, *Bury My Heart at Wounded Knee,* one of the greatest so-called Indian warriors was the Lakota (Sioux) War Chief Tashunka Witco, known to the white man as Crazy Horse. According to Lakota tradition, Crazy Horse's father was an Oglala medicine man who gave his son "strong powers." Crazy Horse first went to war at the age of twelve in response to the slash-and-burn attacks used by U.S. Army General Harney during his punitive 1855 expedition against the Sioux.

As a young man, Crazy Horse meditated regularly and had visions. According to oral traditions, he had a powerful vision of a young rider in a storm with long, unbraided hair with the feather of a red hawk in it, a smooth stone behind one ear, and lightning zigzags painted on one cheek and hail dotted all over him. (Lightning and hail were recognized by the Lakota as powerful natural phenomena.) People gathered around him and clung to him. Soon the storm lifted, and a red hawk flew over the rider's head.

When he awoke from the vision, Crazy Horse recognized that he'd received an important message, and from that time forward, when he dressed for battle, he painted his shield and his body with lightning and hail symbols in the way of the warrior in his dream.

Amazingly, Crazy Horse led his warriors into battle off and on for twenty years—against Generals Crook, Miles, and Custer—without being wounded. He was finally killed by a soldier's bayonet in 1877 after he surrendered and was already in the army's custody.[4]

According to Dee Brown's Sioux sources, Crazy Horse is said to have "dreamed himself" into the real world in 1876, and he showed his people many strategies and techniques to use when fighting the white man's soldiers. For example, when General Crook sent his pony soldiers in mounted charges against the Sioux, instead of rushing forward into the fire of their carbines, Crazy Horse had his men fade off to their flanks to strike weak places in their lines. Also, he kept his warriors mounted and moving from one place to another. By the time the sun was directly overhead, he had the soldiers mixed up in three separate fights. Thus, the Sioux were able to keep the soldiers apart and on the defensive.

As demonstrated by Crazy Horse, Native American warfare practices extended beyond simple technique. The warriors also called upon "powers" from other sources. It's often repeated in Native American ceremonies and prayers: "The bear is stronger, the deer swifter, the eagle more far seeing than us. We are without power; have pity on us." So native people find the power somewhere else: in "medicine," a name for power that comes from mystical sources.

Every tribe has its own way of preparing for war, finding power, and receiving good medicine as protection in battle. Very often, these quests involved visiting physical places, which were considered sacred—places with natural power or a connection to the creator.

The Apache and the Navajo had their sacred mountain where they went to fast and pray, or a river could be a place to find powerful medicine. Objects such as bones and claws that came from animals with respected abilities could also provide medicine in battle. The Cheyenne warrior Brave Wolf was given a mounted hawk after fasting and prayer, which he wore on his head when going into battle. On a charge, the bird seemed to come to life, and Brave Wolf would plunge right into the middle of the enemy, knowing the bird was helping and protecting him.

In the days before the gun came to Indians, shields made of stretched buffalo hide offered some physical protection in war. But the protection with which these shields were endowed went far beyond the physical buffalo hide. The shield was believed to possess mystical powers, and not just anybody could make one. After much fasting and spiritual questing, a warrior was spiritually shown what designs and patterns to use on his shield.

Sioux shields carried images of lightning to capture its destructive powers and often included images of swift, powerful, and respected animals—buffalo, bear, elks, and horses.

Kiowa writer N. Scott Momaday recalled a legendary shield belonging to one of his Kiowa ancestors. In the summer of 1992, Momaday arrived in Oklahoma just after Sitting Bear's shield was returned to his people. Sitting Bear was one of the Qkoie-Tsain-Gah, the ten bravest of the Kiowa warrior societies, who lived from 1800 to 1871. He had been a great chief and a brave warrior.

After much success in battle during the 1860s, Sitting Bear was captured by the army and taken in chains to Fort Sill, Oklahoma. His shield was taken from him when he was captured. Later, he was to be removed from Fort Sill with three other Kiowa warriors, and they all were loaded into the back of a wagon.

As they rode in the wagon, Sitting Bear began to sing the death song of the warrior society, which upset the other warriors. They said he should not sing the song, because the white men would hear. Historically, Native Americans often tried to keep their sacred practices from the prying eyes and ears of outsiders for fear that the outsider might steal a person's power by duplicating his words or actions, or, in this case, singing his death song. Sitting Bear told them he was singing the song because he was going to die soon, when the wagon reached a large tree up ahead.

When they reached the tree, Sitting Bear grabbed the wagon driver's hunting knife with his shackled hands and plunged it into the man's leg. Accompanying soldiers shot him dead, and he is buried close to Fort Sill, near that tree. Sitting Bear's shield was taken to New Jersey and kept by the family of the cavalry officer who had taken Sitting Bear captive, until that summer of 1992, when the officer's family returned it to the tribe.

Tribal legend said the shield possessed much supernatural power, so much so the women gathered around it when it arrived, fearing the men would either withdraw its great power or be harmed by it. That shield is said to now be in a safe place where its power cannot fall into the wrong hands.

(Author's note: I can attest to the "power" of the shields referred to in these paragraphs. When researching material for this book, I traveled to the Heye Foundation Museum of the American Indian, located in New York City, and was granted access to their Plains Indian collection. I entered the large room that housed thousands of Native American cultural items collected by George Gustav Heye in his travels near the end of the nineteenth century. In drawers and on a large set of shelves in the center of the room

were century-old Plains Indian war shields, bows, arrows, medicine bundles, and other items. When I opened the first drawer to peek at the items held within, a palpable, yet invisible, force emanating from the objects hit me squarely in the chest. I stepped back. It was as if the objects themselves were warning me not to handle them, for my own sake. Each time I opened a drawer, I felt the same force projecting out, and each time I only looked, but did not touch.)

Back at the 4th of July powwow, one of the drum groups pounded out another song for the dancers as our circle of Indian veterans turned their attention to the women.

"Speaking of women," commented Nathan Hart, an Oklahoma Cheyenne veteran, "they have always been a great motivator for warriors. In traditional Indian societies, it was hard to court a girl unless you had proven yourself in battle. A girl's mother would ask a young man what acts of courage he had done. The women would sing songs about a man whose courage had failed him: 'If you are afraid when you charge, and you turn back, the women will eat you'—meaning the women would talk about you so badly it would have been better to die! John Stands-In-Timber's grandfather, a Cheyenne leader of the 1800s, used to tell him that the possibility of having the women sing about you that way made the men ready to do anything," Nathan concluded.

"My mother was half Cheyenne, half Sioux, from Pine Ridge," said Carol Red Cherries, a Northern Cheyenne vet. "According to the stories that my mother and grandmother told me about the old days on the plains, the women were always very protected, and we had a very strict moral code. Traditionally, during warfare women could move the camp at a moment's notice—take down a tepee in about three minutes.

"During the time I was growing up in the 1970s," she continued, "it was still not proper for women to be in positions of leadership, and some of my relations didn't feel right about me joining the military. But I heard about two Cheyenne women that served during World War II, and that's where I got the idea to join up."

"Some of that might be the white man's influence," Nathan replied, smiling. "But Cheyenne women sometimes rode into war with the warriors. There's the story of Chief Comes-In-Sight in the late 1800s, who was rescued by his sister in the battle against General Crook at Rosebud.

"Some of the bravest Cheyenne warriors were riding back and forth in front of the cavalry volley, letting the soldiers shoot at them. Most of the bullets missed them, but Comes-In-Sight's horse was shot when he was halfway across an open area.

"He landed on his feet, zigzagging to dodge the barrage of fire. His sister was riding with the warriors that day, and she saw the soldier scouts start down the hill to kill him. She came on the run, right into the firing—he jumped on her pony behind her and got away. To this day, the Cheyenne call the battle Where the Girl Saved Her Brother."

Ruth Williams, a Navajo veteran of the Gulf War, sat down in the circle. "Then, of course, there is Lozen, the Apache warrior woman," she said. "My tribe, the Navajo, have long been close allies of the Apache—we're related way back. Lozen was a medicine woman and sister of the famous Warm Springs Apache leader Victorio, who evaded the cavalry for many years. He said she was as strong as a man and braver than most. He called her a 'shield to her people.' She wore ammunition belts and fought alongside the men, just like some of the women in Desert Shield or Iraq."

World War II Choctaw veteran Schlict Billy remarked, "The Choctaw always held women in very high regard. They were part of the councils and had equal freedom with the men. But we always tried to avoid warfare with neighboring tribes in the past.

"Our ancestors set up these inter-tribal stick ball games—it was real serious playing, but it kept us from fighting and killing each other. In fact, we called the stick ball game 'the little brother of war,' and we settled our differences that way whenever we could. But there wasn't a whole lot to fight over in those days; there was plenty of fields for growing corn, good fishing in the rivers, and lots of open hunting ground—so we played hard in the games to get out any resentments."

The Pueblo Indians of New Mexico also preferred to avoid war whenever possible. Made up of Tiwa, Tewa, Towa, and Keres tribes, the Pueblo people tended to stay in their own villages and mind their own business, according to Pueblo historian and anthropologist Alfonso Ortiz. Their

War Captains were more concerned with keeping the religious rules of the community than going to war.

Of course, they defended themselves against raids by the Navajo, Comanche, and Apache, who made a regular practice of attacking the sedentary Pueblo people, but by and large, they were concerned with growing their corn and raising their children. After the Spanish conquistadors arrived at the end of the sixteenth century, however, pueblo life would never be the same.

The Spaniards had steel, gunpowder, and horses, making them formidably equipped invaders. They destroyed Pueblo religious ceremonials, which they considered devil worship, burned their spiritual leaders at the stake in the plaza of Santa Fe, and took their women and children into slavery. In Pueblo belief, a person cannot perpetrate such evil without suffering the consequences, and sure enough, a terrible drought ensued that affected both Pueblo and Spaniard alike.

The Spanish took whatever corn the Indians were able to produce from the parched soil, leaving the people weak and starving. But the Pueblos are patient people, and, thinking that the Spaniards surely must see what was happening, Pueblo leaders waited for the wrongdoers to come to their senses. When it looked like that wasn't going to happen, they finally took up arms and fought.

A spiritual man named Popé from San Juan Pueblo planned a complex strategy from the Kiva (religious center) at Taos Pueblo. Although representatives of the four Pueblo tribes in attendance at Popé's planning meeting did not speak the same language, he devised a system of communication that employed knots tied in ropes and long-distance Pueblo runners. Once the decision to go to war had been made, Popé gave each of four runners a rope tied with the same number of knots. The knots marked the number of days until all the Pueblos were to simultaneously attack their oppressors.

On the appointed day—and with little other than bows and arrows, clubs, and a few captured guns—the Pueblo people surprised the Spanish and successfully evicted them from Pueblo lands. The year was 1680, and it could be considered the first American Revolution. The Pueblo people were fighting for freedom of religion and self-determination.

When speaking of American Indian war practices, the subject often turns to scalping, because this issue looms large in the public perception of Indian warfare. There are many opposing views of the origins of scalping among American Indians. The conventional view is that it was a gruesome practice unique to American Indians, but forms of beheading and scalping have been practiced by societies all over the world.

Some scholars claim that scalping on the American continent was actually introduced by the Europeans, referring to notices published in the 1600s by the Dutch and British colonial authorities advertising a bounty to be paid for Indian scalps. Whatever its origin, the taking of heads or "human pelts" certainly seems to have arrived late on the North American continent, because archaeological sites reveal little evidence of the practice before the 1600s.

As early as 1637, the English colonists of Connecticut offered the Mohegan Indians a bounty for every Pequot Indian head delivered to them, capitalizing on an inter-tribal dispute that had turned violent. The plan also happened to aid the English in their competition with the Dutch for regional natural resources.

Later, in 1675, authorities in the colony of Massachusetts were offering colonists a bounty for what they called Indian "head skins," later also called "redskins." The French got into the scalp trade as well in colonial times.

In the next century, in the American Southwest, the Mexican Army offered high bounties on Apache scalps—women and children alike. One general collected the ears of Apache warriors on a string in his office.

As if the practice of scalping wasn't bad enough, the mutilation of defeated enemies and the collection of "human war trophies" also came into popular practice. However, in the 1800s, members of the U.S. cavalry seemed to take particular pride in this activity, cutting out Indian women's private parts and displaying them like military regalia.

Whether scalping was originally an American Indian practice or not, evidence suggests that it was taken to excess after, and probably as a result of, European contact. Also, it was odd that what became known as the Indian practice of scalping should be met with such horror by the British—who for centuries beheaded political prisoners and stuck their heads on pikes over London Bridge until they rotted off—and by the French, whose republicans made great show of weaving souvenirs of locks of hair from the basket of aristocratic heads severed by the guillotine. The truth of the matter is that most of the world's cultures have exhibited barbaric practices at one time or another.

A war-related practice that does come from Native American tradition is known as "counting coup." The term is of French origin from the verb *couper*, which means literally to hit or strike. The heart of this practice calls for a warrior to touch an enemy warrior during battle without killing him or being killed.

Barney Old Coyote, a member of the Crow tribe, described the practice. "The Crows spent a lot of time on the warpath, but we weren't interested in killing everybody," he said. "In fact, like a lot of Plains tribes, the bravest thing a warrior could do was 'count coup' on the enemy—touch him without his killing you.

"There were four specific acts you had to perform to be eligible for chieftainship with the Crow Tribe. The first was to count coup. The second was to take an enemy's weapon. The third was to take his horse, and the fourth was to lead a successful war party.

"The white people—they thought we Indians were just dirty horse thieves, but to my way of thinking, stealing horses or sneaking up on an enemy without killing anybody is a better way to make war than to slaughter everybody in sight, which is what the cavalry did. Before the white man came, things were different among the tribes."

Carson Walks-On-Ice, another Crow vet, confirmed Barney's words. "Crows have always fought for this land," he said. "We were raised with traditional stories of counting coup and performing deeds to become a chief. Old Crow guys would come to visit my grandfather, and they'd talk all about the coup they had counted in the old days before they settled on the reservation. In our time, Joe Medicine Crow was the only living Crow to do all four deeds to become a chief during World War Two, but that's a story for later.

"Traditionally," Carson went on, "the Crow went on the warpath only for revenge for an enemy raid or to gain honor. It was never to gain territory or wealth or power. When a warrior came back from a war party, he had to give away most of what he had captured. The more you gave away, the more honor you had. We still do that today."

What Carson is referring to is the continued practice of the "give-away," in which a family that has been honored or blessed in some way gives large quantities of goods to other Indian families in their community. This is sometimes done at powwows, when the dancing stops and the honored family takes over the arena, calling up people who may have helped them in some way during the past year. Hundreds of items, including Indian blankets, shawls, dining flatware, food, and clothing may be distributed during the give-away.

Wrapping up their first round of discussions, our circle of veterans started to disperse as another powwow dance session came to a close.

Before departing, Winnebago veteran Doug Long said, "My grandfather was a veteran of the First World War. My older brother is a veteran of the Second World War. My other brother and I are veterans of the Korean conflict, and I have seven grandsons that were in Desert Storm. That meant my grandsons were now Winnebago warriors. In our tribe, every time you get a new warrior, you add a new eagle feather to the tribe's Eagle Staff. So we added seven more feathers to our Eagle Staff.

"I remember that ceremony. It followed our Winnebago tradition. I offered tobacco, as we were taught by our ancestors, blessed the feathers, and prayed to each of the four directions, so that that good feeling could be shared by everyone who is out there in those directions.

"I'm sure I speak for most Native American veterans when I say I was proud to serve, and I'd serve again."

PART TWO

From Freedom Fighters to Rough Riders

Revolutionary War—*Peace medals such as this one, which depicts George Washington and an American Indian, were often presented to tribal leaders who had sworn allegiance to the United States. (National Museum of the American Indian)*

Civil War—*This hand-written ledger page, on display at the Oneida Tribal Museum proudly lists the names of Oneida veterans who served in the Union Army during the Civil War, such a James Otter and Martin Doxtator. (photo by Gary Robinson)*

Civil War—*Cherokee Stand Watie served as a brigadier general for the Confederacy. (National Archives)*

Civil War—*Seneca Chief Do-ne-ho-ga-wa, known as Ely S. Parker among the whites, served as General Grant's adjutant (secretary) and drew up the terms of General Lee's surrender at Appomattox. (Smithsonian Institution National Anthropological Archives)*

Indian Wars—*This Crow Indian Scout named Curley served in General George Armstrong Custer's 7th Cavalry, but survived the Battle of the Little Bighorn. (National Archives)*

Army   Scouts—*Apache Scout William Major posed for this photo with an officer of the 25th Infantry in the 1930s. Though the Army Scouts saw most of their service in the 1800s, the unit was revived for WWI service under General Pershing. (U.S. Army Photo)*

PART TWO—FROM FREEDOM FIGHTERS TO ROUGH RIDERS

The Oneida Tribal Museum, located a few miles west of Green Bay, Wisconsin, is filled with wartime memorabilia, letters, and photographs collected from Oneida tribal vets and their families, who want people to know of their proud military service.

Oneida tribal members living today are proud of the fact that members of their tribe have served in every war America has fought from the Revolutionary War until modern times. That's a remarkable accomplishment when you consider what this and other tribes suffered at the hands of the American government and its citizens.

Members of tribes all across the United States are proud of their veterans and their past and present military service. Every veteran has his memories, and every war has its stories.

The Revolutionary War

It's a fact that most of the tribes in the Northeast sided with the British during the Revolutionary War. The reasons for this are clear.

The colonists were increasingly encroaching on Indian territory, breaking agreements that protected Indian lands. Many tribes had long-standing treaties with the British Crown, which included trading treaties on which the tribes had become dependent. To all the tribes, treaties were not just contracts that could be forgotten or broken—they were sacred promises.

There were, however, many instances in which tribes fought with and supported the colonists. The colonists' pleas for freedom against oppression moved some Native Americans to offer help and support, since many of the tribes in New England had themselves been oppressed by France, Britain, and other European powers.

In other cases, friendships and intermarriage had forged deep ties between settler and Indian, which was true for several Northeastern tribes who had been dubbed "praying Indians" by colonists because of their conversion to Christianity.

There were actually several Native American Minutemen, and there were thirteen Delaware Indians in one colonial military company. It is also a matter of U.S. military record that George Washington's aide-de-camp, Simeon Simon, was an Indian, though his tribe is not mentioned.

And then there were the Oneida, a whole tribe that came to the rescue of the colonial rebels at times of dire need.

The Oneida were part of the League of Six Nations of the Iroquois, a confederacy that predated the thirteen colonies by some three hundred years. In fact, that's where the colonies got the idea of a union of states. In 1751, during one of many meetings called to form the union of colonies, Benjamin Franklin told James Parker, "It would be a very strange thing if Six Nations of 'ignorant savages' should be capable of forming a scheme for such a union [the League of Six Nations] and be able to execute it in such a manner, as that it has subsisted ages, and appears indissoluble, and yet a like union should be impracticable for ten or a dozen English colonies."[1]

Officially, the Six Nations had elected to remain neutral during the colonists' Revolutionary War, but all of that soon changed. In January of 1776, Colonial General Schuyler led a raid into Mohawk territory to capture suspected British loyalists. A prominent and well-respected member of that community was taken prisoner, which sent most of the Six Nations over to the side of the British. But the Oneida were closely tied to the settlers in upper New York State, and they stayed neutral—that is, until the British attacked.

Not far from upstate New York's Fort Stanwix were both an Oneida camp and a colonial settlement. In August, 1777, military personnel at the fort got word that the British Army was coming down from Canada to attack. The British plan under General Burgoyne was to converge in Albany and cut the colonies in half.

Both the Oneida and the colonists gathered inside the fort for protection just as the British forces approached. The fort commander, Colonel Peter Gansevoort, refused the terms of surrender offered by the British, and the siege commenced. According to documents in the Oneida Museum, the Oneida men and women at Fort Stanwix aided in driving off the British and their Indian allies who were trying to undermine and blow up the fort. When they learned of the nearby British invasion, American volunteers of the Mohawk Valley rushed west to relieve their besieged comrades at Fort Stanwix. On August 6, 1777, they blundered into an ambush set by the British around a small ravine two miles from the Oneida village of Oriska. A tremendous slaughter of Americans occurred during the opening minutes of the engagement. The survivors, including several Oneidas, gathered around their commander, Nicholas Herkimer, on a plateau west of the ambush ravine. In the ensuing battle, they and their Oneida allies fought the British and Tory Indians to a stalemate.

Of particular interest in this conflict, known as the Battle of Oriska, were the elderly Oneida war chief Hanyery and his wife. Probably in his fifties, Hanyery was said to be "too old for the service." Yet he and other Oneidas fought side-by-side with their American allies on the main plateau of the battlefield.

After the battle, it was reported that Hanyery, who was on horseback, was shot through the right wrist so as to disable him from loading his gun. Subsequently, his wife repeatedly loaded it for him, and he managed to continue firing. His wife also had a gun, which she used in the fight.

The details of this battle were confirmed by a local newspaper, which noted that Chief Hanyery and his wife "distinguished themselves remarkably on the occasion. The Indian killed nine of the enemy, when having receiving a ball through his wrist that disabled him from using his gun, he then fought with his tomahawk. His son killed two, and his wife on horseback fought by his side with pistols during the whole action, which lasted six hours."[2]

The Oneida immediately moved on to Fort Saratoga, where they helped defeat the British in the battle that is considered the turning point of the Revolutionary War. By that time, the Oneidas had officially been enlisted into George Washington's Continental Army.

According to Oneida records, the then leader of the Oneidas, Chief Shenandoah, sent hundreds of bushels of dried corn to feed George Washington's army during the terrible winter of 1777–78 at Valley Forge. An Oneida woman, Polly Cooper, even showed the soldiers how to cook the corn. Martha Washington gave her a shawl as thanks. That shawl resides in the Oneida Tribal Museum to this day, alongside a letter from George Washington in which he writes that his soldiers would have died of starvation if it hadn't been for the Indians' corn.

One of Washington's surgeons at Valley Forge, a Dr. Waldo, wrote in one of his reports, "I was called to relieve a soldier thought to be dying. He expired before I reached the hut. He was an Indian, an excellent soldier, and had fought for the very people who disinherited his forefathers."[3]

When, many years after that winter at Valley Forge, Washington was concerned about the British advancing position, he turned for help to his French aide, Marquis de Lafayette, a French citizen who'd come of his own volition to aid the Americans in their fight for freedom. Washington sent Lafayette across the Delaware River with some of his troops, including a whole contingent of Oneidas.

As the British forces approached, Lafayette found himself and his forces surrounded, with their backs to the river. There was one chance to cross at a low place in the river, so LaFayette sent 150 Oneidas to hold off the British, while the rest of his troops crossed the river to safety. When the British Cavalry arrived in the vanguard, the Oneidas let out blood-curdling war whoops, which spooked the horses, and they threw all the officers.

The British infantry coming behind didn't know what was going on, and chaos ensued long enough for Lafayette's men to get across and the Oneida to escape without a scratch, as well.

The Colonists always promised the Oneidas would participate equally in all the good things that would come after the war, including land, food, money, and integration into American society. General Philip Schuyler even wrote to the Oneida people, "Sooner would a mother forget her child than we shall forget you."

But when the war was over, the colonials left the Oneidas with nothing, blaming all Indians for the fact that many had fought on the side of the British. Oneida villages and fields and all they owned had been destroyed during the war, and they lived as refugees on the banks of the Mohawk River, their crops burned, the game killed or scared off, and with no relief from the fledgling U.S. government.

White squatters, settlers, and speculators began pouring into Oneida country by the thousands at war's end, and instead of assisting their former allies, the New York state government moved quickly to dispossess the Oneidas of their territory. The state claimed these lands for several reasons. Some Indian tracts had been promised to veterans as bounties in place of pay, and the state's plan for economic recovery was largely based on income from the sale of Indian lands.

But most importantly, the government of New York wanted a population of non-Indian farmers who would be expected to expand and defend the borders of the state while taming wilderness and paying taxes. New York acquired most of the Oneidas' land in a series of forced land cessions beginning in 1785.

It took the Oneida another ten years of petitioning the U.S. government before they were able to sign a treaty that included an official "thank-you" for their service in the war, small compensation for lost land and the promise that they could keep their remaining lands forever. As a result of this treaty, the Oneidas have fought for the United States in every major war since then.

Red Sticks and the War of 1812

When the British and Americans went to war again in 1812, the Muscogee (Creek) Nation, occupying large portions of Alabama and Georgia, decided to remain neutral. This resolve changed, however, when American settlers began aggressively moving in on their tribal lands in violation of existing treaties.

The British played some heavy politics and convinced the Creeks that it was in their interest to fight with the British against the Americans.

When the Creeks held a War Council and decided to go to war, it was their custom to send a bundle of sticks painted red to nearby villages to mark the number of days until warfare would begin. Thus, these Indians were dubbed the Red Sticks.

The tribesmen hoped the British might honor their treaties better than the Americans had, and offered their allegiance. But promises were made on the other side too. Pro-American Creeks and members of other tribes, including some six hundred Cherokee, were recruited to fight under General Andrew Jackson, later to become president, declaring that they were "all fighting under one cause." Jackson attempted to wipe out the Red Sticks first by using only the Indian soldiers, but wholesale slaughter was not the Indian way to make war. Jackson finally brought in his white troops. By the battle's end, only seventy of the nine hundred Red Sticks were left alive. Half of Jackson's casualties were his Indian auxiliaries.

Jackson revealed his true feelings for his Indian troops to Thomas Pinckney, then fighting as a general alongside Jackson. He told Pinckney that he'd rid himself of the Indians at the earliest possible opportunity. Jackson made his feelings public when, after his inauguration as president in 1829, he announced that he had no intention of honoring treaty obligations to the tribes. Jackson pushed his Indian Removal Act through Congress in 1830, in which the majority of the tribes of the Southeast—including the Cherokee who had fought and died under his command—would be removed from their ancestral lands to territory west of the Mississippi.

The Choctaw were the first to be driven on the long trek from their ancestral homelands in Alabama and Georgia to a place called "Indian Territory" (now Oklahoma). Under guard of U.S. Army troops, they were forced to walk through blizzards and freezing weather. Many of the Choctaw were barefoot and starving. The Creek Indians were next, many of them in chains. Nearly half the Creek Nation died. The Cherokee were next, losing a quarter of their numbers to sickness and exposure. Still others were to follow. The path that each of these tribes took became known as the Trail of Tears.

"We never had a thought of exchanging our land for any other ... it being the land of our forefathers.... Fearing the consequences may be similar to transplanting an old tree, which would wither and die away, and we are fearful we would come to the same," said Levi Colbert, a Chickasaw.[4]

The Civil War

Though most tribes tried to remain neutral during America's War Between the States, many natives, including entire Indian regiments, ended up fighting on both sides.

The U.S. War Department, as well as a number of individual career officers, initially opposed the enlistment of Indian troops. Aside from considering Indians the enemy, they feared that Indians would "revert to savagery" in battle.

But as the war continued, and realizing the stronghold the Confederates were gaining with the tribes in Indian Territory, the War Department began to soften its position. For many Indians, the Union government was still the enemy. It had, after all, removed them from their ancestral lands and placed them on reservations. So when the Union leaders asked the tribes to become allies, most were unresponsive. The first inclination among the majority of tribal leaders was to stay out of the white man's war.

However, several minority splinter groups within some of the Southeastern tribes (Cherokees, Choctaws, and Creeks) considered the possibility that the Confederate government might be more honorable than the one they currently had to deal with, and this swayed the loyalties of some Indian people.

The Trail of Tears had created rifts and factions among many of the eastern tribes, which were now in Indian Territory (Oklahoma). There were those who would rather die than leave their land, and they stayed behind, often hiding out in the mountains or forests to escape capture. Others, who felt that a sacred agreement must never be broken, no matter how the other party behaved, had agreed to be relocated.

The Confederates offered the tribes new treaties and promised that the Indian regiments would be mobilized only if there was action in Indian Territory. And, for the first time, several Indians were offered commissions as officers in the Army—the Confederate Army.

The Union, on the other hand, only offered the tribes a wartime reduction in the already meager rations that had been promised at the time of removal. Some tribes, nonetheless, chose to honor the treaties in place with the federal government and agreed to form Indian regiments within the Union Army, with white officers in command.

So the rosters of Confederate Indian forces grew, with outfits called the Creek Mounted Rifles, the 1st and 2nd Cherokee, the Seminole Battalion, and others. Even the Kiowa and the Comanche, still roaming the plains of Oklahoma and Texas, agreed to participate in the Confederate Army, looking for opportunities to attack a now well-established foe.

The Union armed its Indian regiments badly, the Confederates far worse. Often, the soldiers resorted to bow and arrow and tomahawk rather than the old, useless flintlocks they had been issued. Of greatest irony, they were drilled in the organized style of warfare practiced by the Euro-American forces the Indians had been so successful in defeating in previous wars. But they stood their ground, and the Cherokee, Creek, and Seminole took losses proportionately higher than any state, North or South.

Among those who remained loyal to the Union was Opothleyahola, an eighty-year-old chief of a band of Creek Indians. Because of his refusal to take up the Confederate cause, his band was attacked by Colonel Cooper and his regiment of Confederate soldiers and driven from their homes in Oklahoma. The old Creek chief led his people out of Indian Territory to sanctuary in Union-controlled Kansas. Four thousand, mostly women and children, began the long trek eastward. They were repeatedly attacked in their flight by Colonel Cooper's troops and fought them off successfully with their rearguard defense.

Cooper then ordered the First Cherokee Mounted Rifles to attack the Union loyalists. But attacking a retreating band of Indian men, women, and children who were simply honoring their treaty agreements was not an order the Cherokee could, with honor, carry out. They deserted en masse and eventually joined Opothleyohola as he struggled toward Kansas.

Through the rest of the blood-drenched Civil War, the Indian regiments would gain honors in battle on both sides, and Indian officers earned the highest of medals and promotions, some achieving the rank of brigadier general. This did not, however, stop the popular press from characterizing them as the "Aboriginal Corps of Tomahawkers and Scalpers."[5]

A young white Union soldier, James Newton, wrote from the battlefield, "I was on picket duty one night about three quarters of a mile from camp. I had two Company F Indians. One, a new recruit, couldn't talk or understand our language, and the other had to give him his orders. He was posted in front across the road from the house. When I went to relieve him, he was gone. He had gone into the woods, where he could get out of sight as it was open ground where I had posted him. The Indians were good skirmishers, but didn't like the open country or pitched battle."[6]

Probably the most well-known and most written-about Indian who fought for the Confederacy was Cherokee General Stand Watie who commanded the 1st Indian Brigade. This brigade was composed of Colonel R. C. Park's 1st Cherokee Regiment, Colonel W. P. Adair's 2nd Cherokee Regiment, Major J. A. Scales's Cherokee Battalion, Colonel D. N. McIntosh's 1st Creek Regiment, Colonel Chilly McIntosh's 2nd Creek Regiment, Captain R. Kenard's Creek Squadron, Major Broken Arm's 1st Osage Battalion, and Lt. Colonel John Jumper's 1st Seminole Battalion.

Military reports indicated that whatever the Indian units lacked in military training, weapons, and uniforms they more than made up for in the courage and devotion they showed their cause, whether Blue or Gray. The reports do also show, however, that they disliked the repetitive training and military ceremonies, which for them held no cultural or practical significance. [7]

In a Virginia farmhouse owned by Wilmer McLean in the town of Appomattox Court House, Confederate General Robert E. Lee surrendered to Ulysses S. Grant at the war's end. Grant's adjutant was a Seneca

Indian named Do-ne-ho-ga-wa, better known among whites by his English name, Ely Parker.

Parker had studied law in New York but had been denied admission to the Bar because he was Indian and not a citizen. He then studied engineering and later volunteered for the Union Army but was rebuffed. He wrote, "I had, through the Hon. Wm. H. Seward, personally tendered my services for the non-slaveholding interest. Mr. Seward replied: 'The fight must be made by white men alone. Go home, we will settle our troubles without any Indian aid.'

"But the quarrel of the whites," continued Parker, "was not a wrangle of boys, but a struggle of giants and the country was being wracked to its very foundations. Then came to me in my forest home a paper bearing the great red seal of the War Department. It was an officer's commission in the Army of the United States."[8]

This reversal was due to the intervention of Parker's lifelong friend Ulysses S. Grant. Ely Parker's distinguished service, education, and skill made him such a valuable asset that he was promoted to brigadier general in later years, after the war.

At Appomattox, Parker was at Grant's side, drafting the terms of surrender. Parker remembered, "After Lee had stared at me a moment, he extended his hand and said: 'I am glad to see one real American here.'"[9]

At the end of the Civil War, Indian soldiers and officers of both sides returned to find what little they had devastated. Regardless of how many of a tribe's warriors had fought for, been decorated by, and died for the Union cause, any involvement by *any* tribal members with the Confederates resulted in the whole tribe's subjection to the punitive measures of reconstruction. Tribal lands and property were seized and often sold to the highest bidder. And the great Oklahoma Land Rush of 1895 was made possible through the seizure of Indian lands at the end of the Civil War.

Indian Wars and Indian Scouts

The desire to survive as a people was a basic part of Native American existence in the eighteenth century. It flowed in the veins of native warriors as it had for generations. As a result, Native Americans were not easily ushered from their homelands.

The "Indian Wars" is the name generally used in the United States to describe a long series of conflicts between the U.S. Army and Native Americans from about 1825 to 1890. Much of this action took place in the plains region as white settlers spread out and took control of more and more Indian lands. When the Indian Wars started, the U.S. Army set up forts to defend the white settlers and in the process, took over thousands of acres of Indian territory.

All the Indian people had ever fought for was the right to keep their lands and their ways of life. In essence, they were fighting for homeland security, as Americans do today.

As in Revolutionary War times, some U.S. military personnel realized that if the country was to win the war for more land, it would be necessary to enlist Indian warriors on their side. So on July 28, 1866, an act of Congress established the Indian Scout service to provide "in the territories and Indian country, a force of Indians not to exceed one thousand, to act as Scouts, who shall receive the pay and allowances of cavalry soldiers."[10]

General John Schofield, Secretary of the War Department, wrote that the practice of recruiting Indian scouts for the army "will move these men from the rank of savage enemies to the ranks of friends and practically civilized allies—from the life and character of savage warriors to those of civilized husbandmen."[11]

So, army representatives went to meet with tribal leaders of the various Plains tribes and request that tribal members be allowed to serve in the U.S. Army. Tribal response was mixed. Among the Cheyenne, for example, there was a long deliberation on this request, for there were many related issues to be discussed.

Two factors played a part in the final decision to allow young Cheyenne men to serve. Firstly, said Little Chief and Dull Knife, two Cheyenne leaders of that time, their people must learn a new way of life—leave the old way behind, build schools for the children. They recognized that the Cheyenne would no longer be able to live the way they had once lived.

Secondly, their warriors were among the most feared of the plains at that time. A small remnant had held off several thousand U.S. troops. They were willing to continue fighting and would have, but they saw a more pressing need to preserve life for their children and give the elders an opportunity to live out their last days with their grandchildren.

These same warriors laid down their weapons so that their young people and their elders could receive food, clothing, and other aid. Thus, a large number of Cheyenne enlisted and were used as scouts to track down Chief Joseph of the Nez Perce during his well-known flight toward Canada.

But there were also dissenting warriors who fired their guns in the air and called Dull Knife "a white man's woman" when he made the decision to cooperate with the army. These warriors were among those who prolonged the Indian Wars into the 1890s.

Many warriors from the Cheyenne, Crow, and other Plains tribes served honorably as Army Scouts. By 1867, there were four hundred seventy four Indian Scouts, and twenty years later, they reached their peak number of six hundred.

For the first thirty years of the scouts' existence, their enlistment was for only six months at a time, as is evident from the following facts recorded in military discharge papers: "Know ye, that Run-All-Over-the-Ground, a Private of the 5th U.S. Mounted Infantry of Enlisted Indian Scouts, who was enrolled on the First day of August one thousand eight hundred and eighty to serve six months is hereby discharged from the service of the U.S. Army. Character: Excellent. Paid in full $25.68 at Ft. Keogh, Montana, February 15, 1881."[12]

During the Nez Perce War of the mid-1860s, Lieutenant Hugh Scott commanded thirty-five Northern Cheyenne Scouts, men who had recently surrendered to the army. Some of Scott's colleagues warned him of the Indians' capacity for treachery. Scott emphatically differed. He said, "These Scouts are keen athletic young men, real specimens of manhood—more than any body of men I have every seen before or since. They just knew what to do in every emergency and when to do it, without any confusion or lost motion. I watched their every move and learned lessons from them that later saved my life."[13]

While on duty, Indian Scouts wore the same uniforms as regular soldiers, except for their footwear, which were the Apache-style buckskin moccasins that extended above the calf with hard soles turned up at the toe. For a period of time, the scouts were distinguished by a patch on the front of their hats made up of the letters U.S.S. (United States Scouts) above a pair of crossed arrows. Often, however, before going into battle, they would strip down to loincloths and cover their heads with bandanas to differentiate themselves from the hostile Indians on the field.

Indian Scouts were so immensely useful to the army because of their experience and mastery of hunting and warfare techniques. They were the fastest runners, the toughest riders, and the most quick-witted, and they were honored for being so.

Of the Indian Scouts, one army field captain wrote, "A few such men as the Delawares, attached to a company of troops upon the Indian frontier would, by their knowledge of Indian character and habits, and their wonderful powers of judging the country, following tracks (which soldiers cannot be taught), enable us to operate to much better advantage.... [They are] intelligent, brave, reliable and in every aspect well qualified."[14]

As stated earlier, the hiring of Indian scouts by the army to hunt down and often kill members of those tribes and factions of tribes who resisted confinement to reservations was a source of some controversy. Even now it is hard for many people to understand how the descendants of Apache Army Scouts, for instance, take pride that their ancestors helped capture Geronimo.

In order to understand this, you have to understand a little of the Indian way of thinking, the Indian idea of honor. Native American culture has tremendous respect for the rights of the individual, even though the societies are close knit and built around extended family units. If a man, or woman, follows an individual vision—the path that person sees as the only one he can take, with integrity and a moral commitment—then that choice must be honored. If he finds that path is not the right one and he has been mistaken, like the Confederate Cherokee units in the Civil War, then he is free to come back to the community, be cleansed, and be welcomed back into the circle.

With few exceptions, traditional Indian peoples are deeply devout. The acknowledgment of a higher power is a profoundly rooted part of native cultures. Life is a balancing act, every action has consequences, and those consequences might require spiritually mandated, follow-up actions aimed at reestablishing the balance.

For example, the taking of a life, human or animal, friend or foe, red or white, is an act that carries with it grave responsibilities and the need for forgiveness. Treaties, therefore, were not just political documents to be manipulated or forgotten when they proved inconvenient. A sacred promise must be kept or the consequences were grave—even if that agreement meant a person must go out to fight his or her own brother.

There is a strong tradition, particularly among the Plains Indians, of the "honorable" enemy—an opposing tribe or band so brave and strong that they make one a stronger warrior, with greater honor, by fighting them. Sometimes, the army was considered an honorable enemy.

General George Crook, in command of Arizona's army forces in the early 1880s, confided in later years that, often, the Indians he had to fight went to war only when pushed beyond normal human endurance by government agencies and white settlers. He said that his men had to fight *against* the Indians when their sympathies were often *with* the Indians.

However, General Crook's views were not shared by the War Department or many of his fellow officers. He was replaced by General Nelson A. Miles, to whom Geronimo finally surrendered.

All of Geronimo's people, the Chiracahua Apache—including the scouts who had served the army—were removed from their Arizona desert to a dank prison in Florida, where disease and confinement brought more death and suffering than the army ever could.

Between 1872 and 1890, sixteen Indian scouts were awarded the Medal of Honor, the highest military decoration of the United States government, for bravery in action during the Indian Wars.

Historians generally consider that the Indian Wars ended with what's known as the Pine Ridge campaign of 1890, culminating in the Wounded Knee Massacre, in which 146 Lakota men, women, and children were killed by the Seventh Cavalry on the Pine Ridge Reservation.[15]

The end of the Indian Wars meant there was less need for scouts in general and brought a dramatic reduction in the number of Indian Scouts. By 1891, there were only twenty-three still on active duty. However, they were temporarily reactivated the following year to serve with General Pershing's punitive expedition into Mexico in pursuit of Mexican revolutionary general Pancho Villa.

In May of 1916, the Indian Scouts fought in their last official battle, which was against Pancho Villa's men at Ojos Azules Ranch, located about three hundred miles inside Mexico.

The last of the Indian Scouts, who were kept in service after Pershing's expedition, were stationed at Fort Huachuca, Arizona, until the unit was disbanded in 1947.

Troop L—An Experiment

The success of the scouts prompted several army officers to recommend, in the 1890s, the creation of all-Indian regular army units similar to units of East Indian soldiers created by the British Army in India.

At the time, there was no general agreement among military leaders as to the fitness of Indians for regular service. As the *New York Times* reported in a story published on December 27, 1893, "It is remarkable how widely officers of experience differ on this matter." The same story went on to quote a report from Army General Schofield, stating that the army service of Indians "has been quite satisfactory—the young Indians become obedient, subordinate and contented soldiers, instead of restless and dangerous elements within their tribes."[16]

Similarly, Army Inspector General Breckingridge, quoted in the same newspaper story, found that Indians under his command were "amenable to discipline, generally of good habits, proud of their occupation, and of great attitude for military service."

However, other high-ranking officers, including General Philip Sheridan and Adjutant General Williams, believed that Indians should only be allowed to serve as scouts and nothing more. Over the objections of General Sheridan and others, the U.S. Army did create a few experimental all-Indian companies. One was known as Troop L, commanded by Lieutenant Hugh L. Scott of the Seventh Cavalry. Scott was known for his understanding of Indians, Indian ways, and even Plains Indian sign language.

According to reports collected by the *New York Times*, Scott's Troop L was praised for "their rapid progress in drill and discipline," and the Indians in that troop were expected to become "among the very best soldiers in the army."

However, in the long run, Indian soldiers did not take well to the regimen and regulation of life in the barracks and became bored with this lifestyle, so alien to their own style of life and warfare. Their hair was chopped off, they slept in barracks and marched in neat rows in constricting uniforms and boots. In contrast, the Indian Scouts were still living and fighting like warriors—and they were paid more.

And so the experiment failed—but the final deathblow for Indian companies was really the refusal of white officers to lead them.

The Rough Riders

The "Rough Riders" was a nickname coined by the American press to refer to the 1st United States Volunteer Cavalry Regiment, formed to fight Spain during the Spanish-American War of 1898. At the outbreak of this war, Theodore Roosevelt was serving as assistant secretary of the Navy. He resigned that position specifically to form this regiment, which began recruiting men in several states, including Oklahoma.

Despite the overt prejudice they faced, a number of Oklahoma Indian men enlisted in this regiment. Mr. Roosevelt had been known to express some fairly harsh views of Native Americans, but of his Rough Riders he remarked, "We have a number of Indians who are excellent riders and seem to be pretty good fellows."[17]

Roosevelt claimed they lived on the same terms as the white soldiers. They served with him in Cuba, in the Philippines, and later, during the Boxer Rebellion, in China. This service seemed to confirm a nation-wide movement known as "assimilation" that sought to bring Native Americans into the social mainstream as soon as possible.

But that was a debate yet to be resolved.

PART THREE

Doughboys and Leathernecks

World War I—*First World War Native American veterans Cecil Gallamore, Rabbit Boney and Ray McDonald stand at attention for this photo. (Mathers Museum of World Cultures, Indiana University.)*

World War II—*The Comanche codetalkers used in Europe are not as well known as their Navajo counterparts but proved to be just as effective in preventing enemy code-breaking. These codetalkers were part of the U.S. Army's 4th Signal Company. (U.S. Army Photo)*

World War II—*Pima Indian Ira Hayes is probably the most publicized American Indian soldier in U.S. history. After participating in the famous flag-raising on Iwo Jima, he and the other men in this photo, toured the United States promoting war bonds. Tragically, Hayes was found dead in a ditch on his reservation shortly after the war. (U.S. Marine Corp Archival Photo)*

PART THREE—DOUGHBOYS AND LEATHERNECKS

During the opening years of the twentieth century, America was engaged in a national debate concerning the fate of Native Americans. The assimilationists, mostly educated whites living on the East Coast, believed that Indians should continue to be mainstreamed in all aspects of life, including clothing, customs, hairstyles, housing, employment, religion, and education. Separatists tended to believe that Indians were incapable of full integration into American society due to their "inferior" nature.

American Indians, it seems, were seldom consulted regarding these issues. Many were eager to prove themselves within the national arena in all walks of life while firmly maintaining their preference for practicing traditional native ways. To indigenous people, the two are not mutually exclusive.

Into this debate stepped retired minister and self-proclaimed academic doctor Joseph K. Dixon, who had been hired as a lecturer for the Wanamaker Department Stores, located in New York and Philadelphia, in 1907. Dixon, whose research and lectures increasingly focused on Native Americans, convinced his employer to finance a series of expeditions into Indian Country to gather educational information on what he believed to be a "vanishing race."

During his expeditions, Dixon discovered the degree of prejudice to which Indians across the country were being subjected. In 1913, he conceived of the idea of creating "The Declaration of Allegiance of American Indians to the United States." With permission from the newly elected President Woodrow Wilson, Dixon traveled to eighty-nine Indian reservations to perform signing ceremonies, in which he obtained 900 signatures representing 189 tribes.

World War I

With America's entry into World War I in 1917, several Indian tribes declared war on Germany independently of the United States, and thousands of Native American men and women volunteered for military service. Initially, they were rejected because they did not speak or read English. However, the efforts of Dixon and others in the Department of the Interior may have influenced the War Department to reconsider.

In the early 1900s, the Department of the Interior operated about twenty-five Indian boarding schools around the country, and, with War Department approval, the schools quickly became recruiting stations. At Virginia's Hampton Institute, one Lakota student, Charles Roy Morsea, gave a patriotic speech to his fellow students encouraging their enlistment. He explained that his father had served earlier, in the Spanish-American War, and was already fighting in France with General Pershing.

Despite a variety of racial, social, and linguistic barriers, more than seventeen thousand Indians saw active service in the army and navy during the First World War. Some two-thirds were volunteers, even though Indians as a whole weren't allowed to become citizens until after the war.

Ironically, the federal policy of assimilation mandated that, with few exceptions, soldiers of the American Indian race were not designated as such, resulting in little official recognition of the accomplishments of this group during the war. But, thankfully, they did not go entirely unnoticed.

To the surprise of many of the commanding officers, Indian soldiers proved adept at learning to use complex equipment and speak other languages. However, their methods were not always orthodox. For example, two Comanche soldiers in a unit, endangered by not knowing the German strategy, devised an unusual plan. They waited until nightfall, stripped down, and covered their bodies completely in whitewash. Under the cover of darkness, they crept out into "No Man's Land" and waited near the enemy lines until daylight. There, they stood absolutely still next to white-washed fence posts, eavesdropping on the enemy communications. They were able to sneak back to their unit and report what they'd heard.

Also, Winnebago vet Douglas Long remembered stories he'd heard growing up of a WWI Winnebago soldier, Henry Decora, and his father, Foster, who had enlisted in the army. Their division took on the Germans on August 3, 1918, and Foster was killed. The unit then crossed the Hendenburgh Line and went on to push the Germans across the Marne River. There, Henry was gassed. He never received any veteran's disability coverage, although he had to have an eye operation as a result of the gassing. When he came back to Minneapolis, he went into a bar for a celebratory drink, but they wouldn't serve him because he was an Indian.

Personal accounts of Native American heroism like these are numerous. There were the daring exploits of Lieutenant Sylvester Long Lance, who took part in many wartime maneuvers and was reported dead four times. Francis Lequier, a Chippewa, was wounded eleven times during the process of capturing a machine gun nest. And a northern California Indian named Philip Jim was noted for leading charges against the enemy thirty times.

The least known and most underappreciated aspect of Native American service during WWI was probably the use made of a tribal language to send coded messages that the Germans never broke. According to a report filed by Army Field Commanding Officer Colonel A. W. Bloor, the Germans were masters at listening in and decoding all U.S. Army field communications during the war in Europe. Every planned battle or maneuver was effectively thwarted by German forces, who obviously knew what was coming. America was losing the war.

It was in 1918 that a group of Choctaw soldiers presented the idea of using their so-called "obsolete" tribal language as a code. Having exhausted every other means of transmitting coded information, military commanders felt it was worth trying. One Choctaw was placed at each of the Allied field camps to send and receive messages in the Choctaw language. The first use of this system came in October of that year, when a delicate withdrawal of two American infantry companies was ordered. When the movement was completed without mishap or injury, Army Command knew it was on to something.

The Indians were used repeatedly throughout the rest of the war, and according to Colonel Bloor's report, "within 24 hours after the Choctaw language was pressed into service, the tide of the battle turned, and in less than 72 hours the Allies were on the full attack."[1] A captured German officer confessed that his intelligence personnel were completely "confused by the Indian language and gained no benefit whatsoever from their wiretaps."[2]

According to tribal records, nineteen Choctaws served in the communication corps as what became known as "codetalkers," though they've never been officially recognized for their contribution by the U.S. government. They were, however, honored by the French government in 1989.[3]

Back home on the reservations, despite the fact that federal money promised for Indian health and education programs was diverted to the war effort, native people went all out to support the war effort, volunteering for the Red Cross and buying Liberty Bonds, even though they were not considered American Citizens.

It was largely due to the military service of American Indians that they were at last deemed worthy of American citizenship on a national scale, with passage of the Indian Citizenship Act, in 1924.

World War II

Of course, America's official entry into WWII came with Japan's attack on Pearl Harbor on December 7, 1942. It was rumored that many Native Americans reported to their nearby induction centers the following day, bearing their own rifles and ready to go to war. This was in spite of the fact that Indians still didn't have the right to vote in six states.

Whether or not that is true, within six months of the Pearl Harbor attack, seventy-five hundred American Indians had enlisted in the military, and the numbers grew steadily throughout the war.

Indians fought in every theater of the war, often assigned to the most dangerous operations or duties. They became bomber pilots, scouts, communications experts, gunners, commandos, and even brigadier generals, as we shall see. By war's end, at least twenty-five thousand Indian men and women had served in the armed forces, far outstripping the numbers, per capita, of those who served from other ethnic groups.

The Office of Indian Affairs, within the Department of the Interior, was very eager during the war years of 1941–45 to document and publicize the efforts and accomplishments of American Indians. As a result, the department's periodical "Indians At Work," which had been covering progressive developments in Indian Country for several years, featured multiple articles and photos about Indians in the military, as well as wartime activities back home on the reservations. The stories always seemed to support the theme that the Indian had indeed become a valuable American citizen, standing shoulder to shoulder with his white brother.

The wartime media, in general, capitalized on the well-accepted, stereotyped images of the American Indian. Newsreels bombarded American audiences with such news stories as "Heap Big Launching"—about the launching of a wartime freighter, which featured Indian dances and the presentation of a Plains Indian war bonnet to Eleanor Roosevelt—and "Dragons Get Heap Big Medicine," documenting the presentation of Laguna Pueblo dances to Chinese Nationalist pilots training at Kirkland Air Force Base in Albuquerque.

To many Indian people, these stereotyped portrayals were often puzzling, sometimes offensive. Seldom did reporters or media purveyors take time to actually research and portray Indians as they really were, rather relying on concepts and images already accepted by mainstream America.

However, both on the front line and on the home front, Indian people *did* throw their meager resources wholeheartedly into supporting the war effort. Tribes and individual Indians purchased U.S. War Bonds in the millions of dollars. Tribal industries were adapted to wartime production, as portrayed in newsreels seen in theaters all across America. One such segment featured women on the Navajo reservation who had applied their sewing talents to the production of insignia patches.

Even tribal lands were turned over outright or leased to the government for military purposes. For example, the Sioux of the Pine Ridge

Reservation in South Dakota openly received a representative of the War Department in 1942 who asked to lease a portion of their lands for use as a gunnery practice range. The tribe was happy to contribute to the war effort and accepted a three-cent-per-acre fee, far below market value, with the promise that the land would be returned at war's end. A portion of the land was finally released back to the tribe some twenty-five years later.

Service with Distinction

From Sicily and Germany to the South Pacific, Native Americans of all tribes served in WWII with distinction, fighting in greater proportionate numbers than any other race and garnering an impressive number of Silver and Bronze Star Medals and Purple Hearts.

Thomas Yallup, a Yakama Indian delegate presenting testimony before Congress in 1945, stated, "As Americans, in fact the original Americans, this war really and truly means something to us. Our young men have gone forth to war and have been cited for bravery just as in 1918. Because we are Indians doesn't mean that we do not have as much at stake in the land as you do. Our stake may not mean so much in dollars, but in respect and feeling it means as much and probably more, because of our religion about the land and its resources."[4]

Crow Indian veteran Joe Medicine Crow surprised himself with his own actions during the Second World War. In retelling the events that had transpired during the war, he realized that he had unconsciously performed all four deeds traditionally required for a Crow warrior to become a chief.

His wartime deeds included running on foot under heavy fire into an enemy camp to perform a military objective (leading a successful war party), stealing an enemy's weapon, capturing several enemy horses, and touching an enemy warrior without harming him or being harmed. This series of military actions earned him the title of chief, according to traditional Crow culture. His full story is recorded in the book *Native American Testimony*, edited by Peter Nabokov.

Codetalkers in WWII

Once again, as in World War I, native languages were used to transmit coded messages that were never broken by the enemy. The Army recruited approximately fifty Native Americans for special native language communication assignments in Europe, and the Marines recruited more than three hundred Navajos for communication duty in the Pacific region.[5]

In Europe, the Army Signal Corps first used a cadre of Comanches to send secret telephone messages up and down the line. But because Hitler had learned of America's use of Indian languages in WWI, he had sent a team of German anthropologists to learn native tongues before the outbreak of WWII. However, the task proved daunting, due to the existence of some three hundred Native American languages. The army safely used the Comanche communicators during their D-Day assault on the beaches of Normandy and in other instances.

As a matter of fact, Indians from nineteen different tribes were used in some capacity for sending and receiving tribally based coded messages during WWI and WWII. The best known and most publicized codetalkers were the Navajo, used in the Pacific against the Japanese. The 2002 motion picture *Windtalkers*, starring Nicolas Cage and Adam Beach, brought aspects of this story to the big screen.

Philip Johnston, who had grown up on the Navajo reservation as the son of a non-Indian missionary, introduced to the Marines the idea of using the Navajo language shortly after the beginning of the war. A civil engineer who'd served in the Army Corps of Engineers during WWI, Johnston read about the use of Comanches in Europe and thought the Navajo language could be put to similar use.

Impressed by a demonstration of Navajo code-talking capabilities arranged by Johnston, the Marine Corps authorized a pilot program using thirty Navajo men. After their successful deployment to various battlefront locations in the Pacific, the Marine Corps officially instituted the codetalker program. Throughout the war, the Navajo codetalkers repeatedly baffled the Japanese during numerous battles. Of the thirty-six hundred or so Navajos who served in all branches of service, about four hundred Navajo Marines served as codetalkers.

Nowhere did the codetalkers shine more brightly than during the famous Battle of Iwo Jima. The United States desperately needed a midway location for a bomber base that would allow for strategic attacks on Japanese military targets. Iwo Jima, a small, desolate island covered with volcanic ash, was that place.

In February, 1945, the U.S. Marines began their invasion of Iwo Jima. Japanese forces were entrenched in almost impenetrable underground bunkers overlooking marine landing sites. During the four-day battle, six Navajo codetalkers transmitted and received more than eight hundred messages without a single error, immeasurably aiding in the final capture of the island.[6]

Almost fifty years later, Navajo codetalker Harold Foster reflected on Navajo history and his years of military service in an interview with the author. "For hundreds of years," he said, "the Navajo lived in our homelands. These lands provided good grazing for our animals and good hunting. In the 1800s, when the Anglos and the army moved in, the Navajo were pushed north, to more arid land. Still, our leaders wished to keep the peace, and the Navajo came to the fort to trade and to race horses with the soldiers.

"Some years later, the government arrived at our villages and took our children away to boarding schools where they could learn to be like white people. When we put our children in those schools it was like giving our hearts up, and when the Superintendent abused our children it hurt us very much. When Navajo children spoke their language in school, they were punished.

"My older brother was at Normandy, and my oldest brother was a codetalker, too," Foster continued. "After I arrived at boot camp, I sat and thought to myself, 'Why, why did I join up?' Then I remembered— I joined because I wanted to defend my people, my parents, my relatives, my reservation, my state, and my country, the United States. That's why most of the Navajo's veterans went into service, to defend their homeland."

After the War

When they returned home, Indian veterans were hailed as heroes and used by military-sponsored P.R. campaigns to strengthen support for the war on the home front.

A classic case of home-front P.R. involving an Indian soldier is the case of Ira Hayes, a Pima Indian born in a one-room adobe house and educated at an Indian boarding school. He joined the marines and became a paratrooper, earning two Bronze Star Medals for gallantry in the South Pacific. On February 23, 1945, Hayes, four other marines, and a navy corpsman raised the Stars and Stripes atop Mount Suribachi on Iwo Jima, and the famous photograph of that event was widely distributed back in the States.

As portrayed in the Clint Eastwood movie *Flags of Our Fathers*, Hayes and the others became celebrities back home and were reassigned to sell U.S. War Bonds stateside. "I want to go back to the Pacific," Hayes told his superiors—combat was easier for him than P.R., and he often said that he didn't feel like a hero. His request to return to active duty was denied, and he turned to the bottle to drown his inner conflict. After discharge, he returned to the reservation to find no jobs and nothing but despair.

On Veterans Day 1954, Hayes was brought to Washington with the two other survivors pictured in that famous photograph of the flag-raising on Iwo Jima. The occasion was the dedication of a 750-foot bronze statue of the photograph. Two months after the dedication, Hayes's body was found in a roadside ditch near his reservation home. He had died from alcoholism and exposure. He was just thirty-two years old.

Many Native American veterans of WWII suffered similar, though less tragic, experiences after the war's end. While they might have been viewed as heroes in their own tribal communities, the American society at large viewed them once again as merely Indians—which was the equivalent of second-class citizens.

Nothing dramatized the postwar experience of unassimilated Indians so pointedly as the crisis that hit the Navajo Nation in the winter of 1947–48. The New Mexico Association of Indian Affairs reported that the "poor economic situation of the Navajo nation is beyond belief—two-thirds of the tribe's total income had been lost." The Navajo returned to a subsistence economy, and the average male was earning less than one hundred dollars a year. The tribes' infant mortality rate was seven times the United States average, and only one in five children of school age could be accommodated by the overcrowded Bureau of Indian Affairs–run school system.

After the war, Indian veterans and war workers alike faced uncertain futures. Thousands had been accepted into white mainstream society, relocating to cities to go to work or serving side by side with Anglo men and women in the military. Many found new stature and respect back in their home communities and reservations. Others found that they no longer seem to fit in among their traditional counterparts and so migrated to the nearest cities looking for work. Whatever the case, World War II had forever changed the way Indian peoples interacted with one another and the larger, non-Indian society.

The rapid integration of Indian citizens into white America became the official goal of federal Indian policy. "Termination" of tribal status became the legislative strategy in the postwar years from 1947–53, and liquidation of tribally owned property a major goal. Meanwhile, individual Indian people were simply trying to survive in a postwar economy.

It was against this backdrop that Indians once again rose up to serve their country when the call came.

The Korean "Police Action"

The Korean War (1950–53) was the first undeclared war the United States ever fought. President Harry S. Truman called it a "police action" when he committed U.S. troops to operations on the Korean Peninsula in June of 1950. The Korean War is also sometimes called "The Forgotten War," but a total of 5,720,000 Americans saw military service during this period.

Unfortunately, no records were kept that made a distinction between Indian and white soldiers, and thus there is no official documentation of the contributions Indians made in this war. However, many Indian vets from the Korean conflict are alive and well and willing to share their war and postwar experiences.

For example, Alex Seowtewa, a Zuni Pueblo Indian artist, fought in Korea as a young man. He remembers the conflict this created within him because of the teachings of his traditional Zuni grandfather. "Never point a gun at a human being," his grandfather had taught, and so Alex had to go completely against his training and conscience to execute what he felt were his duties as an American citizen.

After he fought overseas, he returned to the Zuni reservation, near Gallup, New Mexico, to deal with the results of his *internal* war. His first attempt at coping with the problem was through alcohol. Weekend after weekend, Alex found himself sleeping off another binge in the Gallup drunk tank.

Finally, after an intense session of self-evaluation, following a particularly rough weekend, Alex came to grips with the turmoil in his gut and set himself on a new path. Integrating both the teachings of his grandfather and the experiences of his own life, he constructed a personal philosophy for life in two worlds that allowed him to balance the requirements of one with the demands of the other.

Increasingly, this became the way most Indian people had to learn to function in order to survive in modern America: a balancing act.

For other Native American men at the time, military service merely became a means of economic self-support. Take Ronald Stewart, a Crow Indian vet, for instance. "I joined the army in 1952 at the age of twenty," he said. "I needed a job and really didn't have any skills. After sixteen weeks of basic training, I was sent to the frontline in Korea. I served in the army until 1954 and was discharged. I wasn't treated any different than any of the other soldiers I served with. The only problem I got now is getting into a VA hospital. I go over there and try to get some services, they turn me down. It seems like others can get whatever they want. That kind of bothers me."

In the 1950s, the drive for tribal termination pressed on at the federal level, and several small tribes were officially taken off the federal books.

However, many people inside and out of government circles began viewing this policy as a sneaky way for the federal government to renege on its treaty obligations and responsibilities to Indians, and eventually this policy was abandoned.

Vietnam

As the United States began its involvement in Vietnam in the early 1960s, a new consciousness was developing among a generation of young Americans, including urban-based, politically savvy Indians who had mastered the art of living in two worlds. And as the Vietnam War escalated, the civil rights movement grew in strength, and various ethnic movements such as the Black Panthers became vocal and violent, so did the demands and actions of the newly formed American Indian Movement (AIM).

Indian rights and the recognition of tribal sovereignty were two of the main goals of the AIM organization, contrasting sharply with many federal policies and goals of the time, which continued to view Indians as wards of the government who were to be dictated to rather than listened to.

In spite of mounting conflicts and controversies between tribal peoples and the U.S. government, Indians enlisted in the military for service in Vietnam in record numbers, as in previous wars. Many say they did so because of family traditions going back many generations.

Andrew Lewis, an Indian painter from New Mexico, is one such Vietnam vet. "Everyone in my family has been through the military," he said. "My grandmother was a Red Cross nurse in World War I. My grandfather was a captain in World War I. My uncle was in World War II. My mother was a Red Cross nurse during the Korean War, and my father is a veteran of the Korean War, as well.

"Now, my older brother went into Vietnam in the early '60s. But myself, why I went—I just wanted to go. I had friends who went in. My family had been in, so I might as well go. I wanted to see how my attitude would change in the military life. I was born at home on the Pueblo and didn't have a birth certificate, so I could say I was old enough to enlist. I went in when I was only fourteen years old."

Creek Indian Vietnam veteran Willie Haney of Oklahoma had experiences in the war common to many other Indian vets. He shared these comments in a documentary film about Indian Vietnam vets called *A Time to Heal*, which was produced by the author.

"We have seen movies of the Vietnam War," he said. "Yet our Indian people are not portrayed there. You see the black people, the Hispanic people, the white people, but no Indians are there. Yet every time you'd be out in the field in 'Nam, the first thing an officer would do is say, 'Chief, you take point.' The man may have never lived in the country in his life, but if he was an Indian, it was always, 'Chief, take the point.'"

Haney's comments reflect the stereotypical views that many non-Indians have toward Indians, views often derived from Hollywood westerns. These films frequently depicted Indians with innate tracking and hunting skills that almost bordered on the supernatural, and Indian males are often referred to as "chief," a derogatory use of the word.

Haney continued. "One of the things we realize is that a lot of Indians during 'Nam, or anytime, are usually quiet, kind of set back, which may be one of the reasons that movies don't show too many Indians. But every time we are called upon, Indian people are always there. We want people to know that we, as an Indian people, are always ready to fight for our country. This is our homeland. We give it all we've got."[6]

It is interesting to note that one of the first casualties of Vietnam was a young Navajo volunteer, and one of the most highly decorated Indians of that war was Billy Walkabout, a Cherokee who was awarded the Distinguished Service Cross, five Silver Stars, and five Bronze Stars, and who was wounded six times. However, these are the kinds of facts that went unnoticed by the media and the general public during the Vietnam War years.

Crow vet Carson Walks-Over-Ice remembered one decorated native vet that he personally knew. "The Special Forces had an all-Indian team, an 'A-Team.' No one knew about them because they were strictly hush-hush. They were in Laos, China, Russia, Cambodia, Africa, and Thailand.

There was one guy I knew in that outfit, named Medicine Bull from Ft. Peck. He had six Silver Stars. Out of the twelve that were in that outfit, he was one of only two who made it back. He died several years ago—drank himself to death in Seattle."

Medicine Bull's wartime experience likely was shared by many other native vets, for it was in Vietnam that many Native American soldiers found themselves in a crisis of conscience. It was difficult for many Indian soldiers to deal with the images of villages filled with women and children being burned and routed, simply because they were fighting for their homeland. After all, their own tribal histories were filled with similar stories of native people being killed and forced from their lands.

Like many of their white brethren, they also put their lives on the line for love of homeland, but uniquely, many Indian soldiers began to find it hard to understand how that patriotism brought them to fight indigenous villagers in rice paddies in a tiny country thousands of miles from home who, from all appearances, were no real threat to the American homeland.

Later, after the Vietnam War ended, it also did not escape the notice of Native American veterans that they were not represented in the Vietnam Veterans memorial statue in Washington DC. Consequently over the last few decades, many tribes have erected their own memorials to tribal vets who served in Vietnam.

Coping During Peacetime

In 1981, several American Indian Vietnam vets came together and formed the Vietnam Era Veterans Intertribal Association to help bring recognition and healing to Indian vets from that war. They held the first annual powwow of the association that year in Anadarko, Oklahoma. Since then, tribal chapters of the organization have sprung up all across the country.

John T. McIntosh, a Cherokee Vietnam vet, helped form one of the chapters in Oklahoma, because the organization's goals were very near to his heart. He said, "I'd always wanted to do something like this because

I knew that the Vietnam Veteran had been really short-changed because of what he'd been through, and the way that some of the American people had felt. And I always thought that if there was something that could be done to heal those wounds between the American people and the Vietnam veteran, then I wanted to be a part of it because I was there, and I know there are wounds between myself and the way some of the people feel towards me."[7]

George Whitman, a Yuchi Indian vet, joined the Indian color guard established by the Oklahoma chapter to present the colors at parades, powwows, dedications, and funerals. He commented, "When I put that uniform on, it brings back memories of friends that were [in Vietnam), and some of them that didn't make it back. To me, I'm just carrying on maybe what they would have done if they had come back. It's kind of left up to the ones who did make it back to do these things for the Vietnam veterans.

"It's a good feeling," he went on, "because at most powwows, all the Indians respect veterans. No matter where you go, Indian veterans are always respected. That makes you feel good. It doesn't make you feel like you did something wrong. It makes you feel good out there, like you draw power from it. To me, when I'm out there dancing, it feels like all of nature is coming together and it's giving you power."[8]

George's brother, Richard Ray Whitman, took a stance on the other side of the fence, protesting against the Vietnam War. He joined AIM in the early 1970s and actively took part in the various protests sponsored by that organization against the war and against the American government's treatment of Indians in general. These two brothers' lives took different directions during those years, but each respected the other's right to follow his own conscience.

By war's end, over forty-one thousand American Indians had fought in Vietnam. Many had come face to face with an enemy that resembled themselves: indigenous peoples fighting for the right to determine their own futures. This discovery was added to the already harsh realities of this unpopular war.

Like warriors of old, many returning Indian Vietnam veterans were sincerely welcomed back into their home communities with honor pow-wows and cleansing ceremonies. This is one reason that many Indian vets have not suffered from the "postwar-stress syndrome" experienced by so many other Vietnam veterans. These traditional tribal ceremonies continue in contemporary times to purge the emotional and spiritual wounds of battle and restore the warrior to a harmonious place within the community.

The Gulf War/Operation Desert Storm

Unfortunately, stereotypes and ethnic ignorance about Indians didn't end with the Vietnam War. With over three thousand American Indian soldiers stationed in Kuwait during the Gulf War (1990–91), Marine Brigadier General Richard Neal referred to enemy territory as "Indian Country." This slang military term, obviously left over from the Indian Wars of the 1800s, apparently continued to be used during the Vietnam War and into the Gulf War and was applied to enemy territory in any nation.

Leaders of the National Congress of American Indians, which represents tribal governments all across the United States, immediately asked for an apology from the military for the "offensive, ignorant, and insensitive" comment. A spokesman for the military command in Saudi Arabia explained that "Indian Country" is a term that was used in Vietnam to mean hostile territory, but a Pentagon spokeswoman said that the term had no official definition in military manuals.

Military records, provided by the Pentagon public affairs office, show that approximately twelve thousand Native Americans served in the Middle East during the Gulf War, and possibly as many as twenty-four thousand were serving in all branches of the military just before Desert Storm began.

One thing that was obvious from television and print news coverage of the Gulf War was that an increasing number of women had stepped into combat and combat support roles, a trend reflected within Native American communities, as well.

A review of tribal newspapers of the time reveal that tribal communities all across the United States were intensely involved in ceremonial activities aimed at both honoring their young warriors involved in Operation Desert storm *and* bringing them safely home. It was apparent that patriotism among American Indians was as strong as ever.

Unfortunately, the last soldier killed in combat in that war was Manuel Michael Davila, aged twenty-two, Sioux.

Operation Enduring Freedom

The terrorist attack of 9/11 touched Native Americans, as it did all Americans, deeply and immediately. On that day, more than three hundred tribal leaders from Indian reservations all across the country were gathered for a meeting in Washington DC. Their responses to the fateful events of that day were, of course, a mixture of sorrow, disbelief, and anger.

A press release issued the same day by California's Morongo Band of Mission Indians summed up native reaction. "This is a terrible and sad day in American history," the statement said. "The entire community sends our deepest condolences to the families of the people who lost their lives this morning in the heinous, demented terrorist attacks on the World Trade Center in New York and the Pentagon in Washington, D.C. As in every major crisis that this country has faced, we stand with all of America in offering our resources and support in every way."[9]

Within days, outpourings of native generosity began finding their way to New York City. Four Mohawks drove a van full of urgently needed rescue supplies and cash donations to the City. The Mohegan tribe of Connecticut pledged $1 million to help the victims and families of the tragedy, and hundreds of thousands of dollars came from other gaming tribes around the country.

"Operation Enduring Freedom" was the name assigned to America's first military response to the 9/11 terrorist attacks. The name primarily referred to the war in Afghanistan and the initial search for Al-Qaeda leader Osama bin Laden. The number of Native Americans serving in the military at that time hovered around eighteen thousand, though records don't indicate how many were deployed in Afghanistan.

However, the loss of one of their own was never felt more deeply than during those years following 9/11, years of heightened American patriotism, years that Native Americans seemed to feel a part of the American fabric as never before. That was obvious on one cold December day in 2006 at Mandaree, North Dakota, when Army National Guard Corporal Nathan Goodiron was laid to rest. According to the *Indian Country Today* newspaper, the twenty five-year-old Hidatsu soldier died of wounds received in Afghanistan on Thanksgiving Day.

Approximately fifteen hundred people, including the state's governor, John Hoeven, attended the funeral. Governor Hoeven called Nathan "a true warrior and a true hero; he didn't set out to be a hero, but his principles and his character made him one."[10]

In 2003, Operation Enduring Freedom and the search for bin Laden was given a backseat when America launched its offensive against Sadam Hussein in Iraq.

Operation Iraqi Freedom

As with the war in Vietnam, the war in Iraq became quite controversial, both within and outside of native communities. While most contemporary Indian people support our troops wherever they may be fighting, some do not support the political decisions that bring America into a particular war.

However, no one disputes the fact that, once again, Native Americans responded to the call to duty when, in January 2003, America's invasion of Iraq began.

Private Lori Ann Piestewa, a Hopi from Tuba City, Arizona, came from a family that had a long military tradition, with both father and grandfather having served in the U.S. Army. She was already enlisted in the army and serving in the Quartermaster Corps with her friend Jessica Lynch when their unit was deployed in February of that year. Lori's 507th Army Maintenance Company was a support unit made up primarily of clerks, repairmen, and cooks.

Riding in a Humvee that was part of a caravan of support vehicles, Piestewa and her company became lost during the opening days of the war. They were ambushed in Nasiriyah, in southern Iraq, on March 23, 2003, and their vehicle was struck by a rocket-propelled grenade.

Piestewa and Lynch were severely wounded and taken prisoner. Piestewa died soon afterwards. The rescue mission that later saved Jessica Lynch from captivity became one of the early success stories of the war, but her friend, the Hopi soldier, was rarely mentioned.

Piestewa was awarded the Purple Heart and Prisoner of War Medal, and the army posthumously promoted her from private first class to specialist.

Lynch repeatedly said that Piestewa was the true hero of the ambush and named her daughter Dakota Ann Lynch in honor of her fallen friend, whose own middle name was Ann. Additionally, many agencies honored Piestewa's memory with memorials, including the renaming the offensively named Squaw Peak near Phoenix as Piestewa Peak.[6]

Piestewa was the first woman killed in the Iraq War and is the first Native American woman to die in overseas combat. And unfortunately, she won't be the last.

The Tradition Continues

Through the stories and events recorded in these pages, we've seen that Native Americans continue in the proud warrior traditions practiced by many of their ancestors, despite the ignorance and misunderstanding of their ways demonstrated by the federal government and the American people. Understanding the motives and actions of Indian people has always been hard for the general public, but this has never deterred Native Americans from acting with courage from the heart.

*   *   *

"Native Americans fly the American flag at our homes and display yellow ribbons to show our support for our troops. We will quietly go to our sweat lodges and pray. Our drums will beat to honor our warriors. We will join hands in our circle of prayer as the drumbeat courses through our veins and becomes our heartbeat.

"Tobacco offerings and burning sage will float heavenward to carry our prayers. The pipe will be smoked. Honor songs will be sung. Feathers will be earned. We will fight and we will die, beside non-Indians. As the sirens sound and the bombs fall, we honor our warriors. We will pray for their safety as we pray for peace. Tomorrow depends upon it."

—Native American veteran

PART FOUR

Enemies and Allies:
The Paradox of
Native American Service

Proud units of Native American vet color guards exist all over the United States and present the colors at a variety of Native American gatherings including conferences, powwows and public ceremonies. The color guard pictured here is a unit of Southern Cheyennes from Oklahoma. Photo by the author.

The Native American veteran who owns this tipi proudly displays an American flag at his front door. Photo taken by the author at a powwow in 1992.

This design, displayed on a t-shirt hanging in the Oneida Tribal Museum, demonstrates the pride Native American veterans feel regarding their military service. Photo taken by the author in Oneida, Wisconsin, c. 1992.

PART FOUR—ENEMIES AND ALLIES: THE PARADOX OF NATIVE AMERICAN SERVICE

As alluded to earlier in this book, the reasons Native Americans have volunteered for military service, at a rate that far exceeds other ethnic groups, are complex. Many speak of honor and duty, the same reasons other Americans give. Others talk about tribal traditions that span hundreds of years—the original "homeland security," you might say. Whatever the reasons Native Americans risk their lives to face an enemy, the feelings among Indians regarding service run deep. But who defines the enemy?

According to Sam Keen, author of *Faces of the Enemy*, we often create our enemy. Before the weapons come the images. This is a practice common to world civilizations, from ancient China to the Greeks and Romans. Generation after generation, we find excuses to dehumanize each other, particularly if we wish to justify genocide. We characterize the enemy in very specific ways—as an unjustified aggressor, a faceless, dehumanized stereotype deserving of our violence. This allows us to reserve our rational thought for the tactics we will use to destroy them.

In national propaganda, the enemy may be portrayed as an enemy of God, the agent of the devil. The enemy is portrayed as crude, rude, and uncivilized. The enemy is seen as a torturer, a systematic sadist who delights in inflicting pain. The enemy is rapist, destroyer of motherhood and female honor. And the enemy is cast as a barbarian, of another race and therefore less than human.[1]

Seventy years of Hollywood westerns capitalized on all of these "enemy" images, giving audiences such films as *The Searchers*, *Red River*, and *Arrowhead*, among many others, in which all Indian warriors are depicted as vicious sub-humans intent on torturing, maiming, and brutalizing innocent settlers. John Wayne, Charlton Heston, and other stars made fortunes by playing heroic "saviors" in these films, which validated Anglo-Americans as the rightful heirs to this great land.

However, Hollywood was not the first to dehumanize Native Americans in order to justify conquest and settlement. The process began five hundred years ago with the Spanish, as part of a premeditated campaign to dispossess the indigenous peoples of the Americas of their lands and resources.

R. Brian Ferguson of Rutgers University studied the stories and images generated by the explorers and conquerors who followed Columbus into the New World. He says they often dwelt on lurid stories of unbridled native violence.[2] Because Spanish law made cannibals fair game for immediate enslavement, European explorers often created and disseminated false stories of indigenous cannibal buffets as a pretext and justification for their destruction.

The image of the Native American as brutal savage and the primary antagonist to white heroes became a seminal part of the myth of the Wild West. The vast majority of magazine articles and dime novels that perpetuated this image were written by people who either knew nothing of native peoples or who were serving an agenda to exterminate them.

As a matter of fact, the entire dime-novel publishing industry that flourished from 1860 to about 1915 began when the publishing firm of Beadle & Adams in New York City launched *Malaeska, the Indian Wife of the White Hunter,* by Mrs. Ann S. Stephens. It was the first entry in a series entitled *Beadle's Dime Novels,* and the author of this tale of the "wild frontier" was a stout, fifty-year-old woman who hailed from and had never left New England.

Unfortunately, many of the false images and lurid stories of "savage natives" were accepted as true and became part of our recorded history. The Apache—who in actuality had a well-organized, chaste, deeply devout, and physically clean way of life—were a favorite subject of racist libel in fiction. The Apache were labeled as filthy, devil-worshipping, human-trophy-gathering beasts.

However, because of their constant cleansing in sweat lodges and washing with sand when water was scarce in the desert, it was not the Apache who could be smelled for miles off, but the white mountain men—and it was the mountain men who, in reality, boasted of raping

Indian women and using their severed breasts for purses. But the power of the media was potent even in the last century.

One example of the difference between prejudiced image and reality comes from the writings of military wife Ada Vogdes, who lived with her husband, a general, at an army fort on the plains for a while in the 1870s. Before coming to the fort, she, like so many other ladies living on the eastern seaboard, had heard many tales of the "fiercely savage heathens" of the plains and dreaded her move to the fort. The very thought of living so close to Indians caused her to fear for her life.

When the great Sioux war chiefs, Red Cloud, Red Leaf, and Big Bear came to the fort, her position as the general's wife forced her to interact with and help entertain these visitors. After spending only a brief time with these men, her attitude markedly changed. She wrote that these men were gentlemen filled with grace and dignity, and she spent many delightful hours in their company.[3]

But when a Native American went to war for the United States, whether as a scout for the cavalry or a marine in the Second World War, he found himself surrounded by the echoes of the myths of the savage, yet mystically attuned, warrior. Much of the perpetuated mythology, it turned out, was often used as politically expedient propaganda.

Crow Indian Vietnam vet Carson Walks-Over-Ice was one of many who experienced the stereotyped myth. "One thing that's funny is that Indians are never usually put together in a unit," he said. "I don't know why, but the army has a policy not to put Indians together. In 'Nam, they called me 'chief' and expected me to do the long-range reconnaissance patrol. They thought I could see in the dark and that kind of thing. I told them I was not a chief, but they persisted, because that's the stereotype of the Indian."

Northern Cheyenne vet Joe Walks-Along echoed this experience. He said, "There was a lot of unspoken assumption that an Indian was a natural-born warrior, and so I was selected to go out on patrol regularly. Nobody wanted to go on patrol, because that was so dangerous—you were so close to the enemy. They called me 'chief' a lot, but I'm not really a chief. I'm with the Kit Fox Society [a traditional Cheyenne warrior society], so I'm not a chief."

"When I first got to Nam, I was doing road checks on Highway 1," added Northern Cheyenne Vietnam vet Windfield Russell. "I met this other Indian guy from Anadarko [Oklahoma] and we went out on listening posts in the bush. The commander used to always call us for this kind of duty, because we were Indians, and he thought we were better than those other guys to go out into the jungle; we could detect the enemy better."

Vietnam Marine vet Apesanahkwat of the Menominee tribe recalled, "One time they transferred these guys over to our outfit, and there was an Indian guy in there, named Sherman Swift Eagle. We were out on company maneuvers, up in a mountain range, where we come across some tracks in a riverbed there. I was walking point, so I held up the column, and I was feeling them tracks, you know. The commander came up, and Swift Eagle was right behind me. I looked up at Swift Eagle and said, 'Looks like about forty-five minutes.' Swift Eagle felt in there and he said, 'More like a half-hour.' And that Captain said, 'Goddam, you Indians are good.'

"Me and Swift Eagle just busted out laughing," continued Apesanahkwat, known as A.P. to friends. "Those tracks must have been about three weeks old. That was pretty funny, but typical of the way it was over there. I'll tell you something about every Indian veteran that I know served in Vietnam. They always had us walking point.

"I used to ask my lieutenant, who was a black man: 'You know I'm getting ready to transfer back to the States, how come you're making me walk point? I can't see no better than you.' He says, 'I know that, but these guys feel better with you out there.' So they pretty much evenly divided the Indians among the platoons so each platoon had enough Indians to use as point men.

"They respected what they perceived—that stereotype of a skill we are born with to hear and see and smell and all of that. And sometimes you tried hard to live up to that."

Even as they fought, Indian soldiers were the subject of both ridicule and propaganda. World War II army publicity photos sent to the folks back home often posed Indian soldiers in ridiculous, caricature-like poses that reenacted the stereotypes of Indian warriors. Even today, as we try to bring Native American history closer to what really happened and what tribal American peoples were really like, there is resistance from the image-makers of the dominant culture, because those historical cultural icons are so powerful and so familiar.

As noted in Part One, when it comes time for an Indian warrior to return to his home community, his people have ways to welcome and honor him (or her). In these communities, warfare is acknowledged both as a natural part of life's struggles to protect tribal values and also as a disruption of family and community. While war is forced upon the community and upon an individual, veterans who return are to be honored whether they won or lost the conflict.

Not only should veteran warriors be honored, according to American Indian practice, but they should also be cleansed of the stains of battle and restored to a harmonious position within the community. And, consequently, many tribal cultures include both private and public ceremonies and social customs for doing so. For thousands of veterans and their families who attend powwows, the ceremonies, dances, and commemorations are times of genuine healing and community building.

For the families of Indian war veterans, sharing the stories of wartime struggles and sacrifice are an important part of their personal recovery and survival as a people. Such storytelling is another of the many Indian cultural practices that contribute to the health of both the individual and the community.

Charles Chibitty, a World War II Comanche codetalker and member of the Native American Church talked about the spiritual forces he believed protected him. "When they asked me to be a codetalker, I was proud," he said. "We saved a lot of lives when [the Germans] could not break the code. Before I went overseas, there was one man at home—ever since I was little he always called me son. We went back to his house where his old peyote ground is, and he put four peyote buttons on the ground and prayed—he said God gave us this medicine to use when we need it. 'It's going to take you over there and bring you back,' he said. 'When you get scared, you take one out, chew it little bit and pray.' I felt fear because there was a lot of artillery mortars coming in. I came back— I got wounded, but I came back—that old man's prayers went with me."

For all the hardships and prejudices that Indian soldiers found, they also had an immeasurable advantage. They had "good medicine" and powerful faith in that medicine. For many Indian people, the term "medicine" often refers to a combination of rituals, herbal substances, prayer, and faith that carries power to accomplish something that might include physical or emotional healing, protection, or simply effectiveness in one's endeavors.

Codetalker Harold Foster shared this about his preparation for war, his service and his return: "My Navajo religion is my religion that I'll never forget. They did a protection ceremony for me before I went overseas, and that's what brought me back. And when I got back, they did another one to purify my soul. This one medicine man did that for me. It takes four days. It's called the Enemy Way.

"I did pray many times when I was exposed to danger on the main battle line, as a codetalker and a signal man. I prayed as my mother and father taught me, to the Heavenly Being and to Mother Earth. When I came back, my mother told me, 'Son, since you left, almost every morning I have gone to my sacred hill and prayed, using my sacred corn pollen, that you would come back.' Maybe that is the reason I came back all in one piece."

What follows is the testimony of several Indian veterans who were positively affected by the native rituals and beliefs of their people.

Vietnam vet Harold Barse, one of the founders of the Native American Vietnam Veterans Association, commented, "Tribal societies have known all along that you have to do something in order to bring the warrior back into society, through cleansing ceremonies, sweats, to rid the person of the contamination of war. The Vietnam generation is probably the first generation of Indian vets to be born and raised in the city— not reservation Indians—and we have to make the effort to go back and learn our ways if we want to know anything about them and be able to use them to help us."

Oneida veteran Ted Christjohn said this about his postwar experiences: "After my service, I came back here to the Oneida reservation, but at first I had a very hard time. I went on a two-year binge of drinking. I couldn't handle it, and I ended up in jail. Now I'm going through sweat ceremonies and learning more about my tribe's beliefs, and that helps a lot. I just went through a ceremony up on the Menominee Reservation with those guys up there, what's called a White Feather Ceremony. And that was really something."

Crow Indian vet Eddie Little Light: "My uncles were in the Native American Church, and they held a peyote meeting for me before I went overseas and made me a medicine pouch to carry with me at all times. Carson Walks-Over-Ice and I came back together, and we were honored by the tribe. They held a victory dance during the annual Crow Fair. I had a hard time getting readjusted. I couldn't sleep at night. I almost had a nervous breakdown. I would wake up at night in a cold sweat and start to go outside to do things I had done in 'Nam. I started drinking to help me cope. But I had a Crow uncle who helped me get through it with informal counseling and in the sweats and taking me to powwows."

Fellow Crow veteran William Charles Stewart: "While in Korea, I was a squad leader. My clan uncles held a give-away for me before I left, and one of them sent a little bundle with me to take overseas for protection. They said to bring it back with me and give it back to them.

"After I came back and gave that bundle to him, he told me it was just dirt that he had picked up from the riverbank. But he had stood on the riverbank and prayed in the Indian way and said: 'My nephew is going across the water and will take this dirt and bring it back. When he gets back, I'll return this dirt to the same place I got it from. Thank you.'

"These clan uncles held another give-away for me for making it back. Then they took me into a sweat tipi and prayed for me to purify me. They said they were glad to see me make it back, and they prayed for a better future for me."

As the stories and comments of these veterans attest, the actions, attitudes, and experiences of Native American warriors stand in stark contrast to the stereotypes disseminated and perpetuated by the movies and the media. We all have much to learn from these indigenous men and women who heed the call to service and action.

*   *   *

Just as the Cherokee were removed, in the great Trail of Tears, from their North Carolina homes to the plains of Oklahoma, so has the major contribution of the American Indian veteran been removed from, or never fully included in, the national history of America.

To create the United States, the nation's white forefathers first destroyed the many Indian nations already thriving throughout this land. It is a shameful tale of broken treaties, murderous military campaigns, and near-genocide whose legacy remains visible today in a federal agency, the Department of the Interior's Bureau of Indian Affairs, that willfully mismanaged billions of dollars of funds belonging to the very Native American individuals the agency was created to protect (*Cobell v. U.S. Department of the Interior*).

For those Indian veterans who fought to protect the rights of all Americans, much of the past discrimination within the military finally seems to be coming to an end. Native American Heritage Month (November) is now one of several ethnically and culturally related events to be observed by the U.S. Department of Defense, and attempts to better understand Indian peoples and cultures are evident in all branches of the U.S. military.

Native American people, men and women, will continue to answer America's call to duty and will continue to sacrifice and serve, in hopes that one day all Americans—black, white, red, and yellow—will truly be treated as equals.

APPENDIX I
Profiles in Service

PROFILES IN SERVICE

Thousands of Native Americans have served in the armed forces with distinction, and all their stories can't be told in these pages. However, the few men and women profiled here represent a small sampling of the bravery and valor exhibited by Native American soldiers throughout history. The source for the information printed below, except the final entry, is Native Americans and the Military: Today and Yesterday, *published by the U.S. Army Public Affairs Information Branch in March, 1984. This document is reprinted here in its entirety with permission.*

Sgt. I-See-O, Army Scout, 1889–1913

Known as a peacemaker in later life, the man called I-See-O was born near Larned, Kansas about 1851. He enlisted in the Army's unit of Indian Scouts in 1889 at Fort Sill, Oklahoma, and became a courier, messenger and eventually a counselor to Major General Nelson A. Miles.

In his early days at Fort Sill, the Scout met Lt. Hugh Scott, and the two became friends. Later they traveled together in that region wherever conflict developed between tribes or between Indians and whites. Indians came to trust I-See-O's advice and respected Lt. Scott's fairness. I-See-O is credited with preventing much bloodshed on both sides.

When I-See-O retired from military service in 1913, Scott, now Major General Scott and Chief of Staff of the Army, arranged for I-See-O to receive a pension for the rest of his life.

In a letter to I-See-O written in 1919, Scott said, "You and I worked well together at that time, and the Indian people of Oklahoma owe you a great deal of thanks … You and I together brought all those Oklahoma tribes through the same troubles which brought about the death of so many Sioux Indians without firing a single shot, so the white people owe much to you as do your own people."

I-See-O died on March 10, 1927, and was buried in his uniform as he had requested.

Sgt. William Major, Apache Scout
Recipient of the Expert Marksman Badge

Apache Indian William Major enlisted in the Army at Fort Apache in 1921. During his 27 years of service, he was a carpenter, truck driver, and military policeman. As was the practice for many Indian Scouts, Major also hunted deer to supplement the soldiers' diet.

Sgt. Major earned the Expert Marksman Badge by hitting a bulls-eye target with 10 rounds at 500 yards.

He loved the Army and in his later years, loved to tell visitors to the fort about the day he and four other Apache Scouts retired. "It was a fine thing," he is reported to have said. "We rode our horses in review, and they all saluted us. Now I am the only one living."

The Sergeant was indeed one of the last Apache Scouts to serve at Fort Huachuca, Arizona. He died in 1983.

Major General Clarence L. Tinker, Osage
Recipient of the Soldier's Medal

Clarence Tinker was born in 1887 near Pawhuska, Oklahoma, to an Osage father and German mother and grew up speaking both the Osage and English languages.

By 1922, he was a Commanding Officer in charge of the 16th Squadron stationed at Fort Riley, Kansas. He went on to eight other post commands during is military career. While serving in London in 1926, he earned the Soldier's Medal for rescuing a naval attaché from a burning plane, and in 1927, he assisted the Army in creating routes for airmail.

Major General Tinker was lost in action near Pearl Harbor, Hawaii, on June 7, 1942, while leading a squadron of bombers on a mission against the Japanese. At the time he was Commander of the Army Air Forces in Hawaii.

The Oklahoma City Air Depot was renamed "Tinker Field" in October of that year to honor "a gallant and courageous soldier and airman who brought credit to his forbears, his state and his nation." Five years later the air field's name was changed again to Tinker Air Force Base.

General Tinker was inducted into the National American Indian Hall of Fame located in Anadarko, Oklahoma, in 1966.

Jack C. Montgomery, Oklahoma Cherokee Congressional Medal of Honor Recipient

Born in Long, Oklahoma, Jack Montgomery entered the Army at Sallisaw, Oklahoma, and reached the rank of First Lieutenant in the 45th Infantry Division. The deeds for which he was awarded the Medal of Honor occurred during combat in Italy in 1945.

His Medal of Honor Citation reads: For conspicuous gallantry and intrepidity at risk of life above and beyond the call of duty on 22 Feb. 1944, near Padiglione, Italy. Two hours before daybreak a strong force of enemy infantry established themselves in three echelons at 50 yards, 100 yards, and 300 yards respectively in front of the rifle platoons commanded by Lt. Montgomery. The closest position, consisting of four machine guns and one mortar, threatened the immediate security of the platoon position.

Seizing an M1 rifle and several hand grenades, Lt. Montgomery crawled up a ditch to within grenade range of the enemy. Then, climbing boldly onto a little mound, he fired his rifle and threw his grenades so accurately that he killed eight of the enemy and captured four more.

Returning to his platoon, he called for artillery fire on a house, in and around which he suspected that the majority of the enemy had entrenched themselves. Arming himself with a carbine, he proceeded along the shallow ditch, as withering fire from the riflemen and machine gunners in the second position was concentrated on him. He attacked this position with such fury that seven of the enemy surrendered to him, and both machine guns were silenced. Three German dead were found in the vicinity later that morning.

Lt. Montgomery continued boldly toward the house, 300 yards from his platoon position. It was now daylight, and the enemy observation was excellent across the flat open terrain, which led to Lt. Montgomery's objective. When the artillery barrage had lifted, Lt. Montgomery ran fearlessly toward the strongly defended position.

As the enemy started streaming out of the house, Lt. Montgomery, unafraid of treacherous snipers, exposed himself daringly to assemble the surrendering enemy and send them to the rear.

His fearless, aggressive and intrepid actions that morning accounted for a total of 11 enemy dead, 32 prisoners and an unknown number of wounded. That night, while aiding an adjacent unit to repulse a counter-attack, he was struck by mortar fragments and seriously wounded.

The selflessness and courage exhibited by Lt. Montgomery in alone attacking three strong enemy positions inspired his men to a degree beyond estimation.

Ernest Childers, Oklahoma Creek Indian Congressional Medal of Honor Recipient

Oklahoma Creek Indian Ernest Childers was born in Broken Arrow and reached the rank of Second Lieutenant in the Army's 45th Infantry Division. His 1943 Medal of Honor Citation reads: For conspicuous gallantry and intrepidity above and beyond the call of duty in action on 22 Sept. 1943 at Oliveto, Italy.

Although Lt. Childers had previously just suffered a fractured instep he, with eight enlisted men, advanced up a hill toward enemy machine-gun nests. The group advanced to a rock wall overlooking a cornfield and Lt. Childers ordered a base of fire laid across the field so that he could advance. When he was fired upon by two enemy snipers from a nearby house, he killed both of them.

He moved behind the machine-gun nests and killed all occupants of the nearest one. He continued toward the second one and threw rocks into it. When the two occupants of the nest raised up, he shot one. The other was killed by one of the eight enlisted men.

Lt. Childers continued his advance toward a house farther up the hill and, single-handed, captured an enemy mortar observer. The exceptional leadership, initiative, calmness under fire, and conspicuous gallantry displayed by Lt. Childers were an inspiration to his men.

Admiral Joseph J. Clark, Oklahoma Cherokee
Navy Cross and Numerous Decorations

Admiral Joseph "Jocko" Clark, a veteran of three wars, was promoted to the rank of full admiral after receiving numerous battle decorations including the Navy Cross. He retired from the U.S. Navy after 40 years of service.

Clark was born near Pryor, Oklahoma, and graduated from the Naval Academy in 1917. He first served aboard the USS North Carolina during World War I escorting convoys across the Atlantic Ocean. He then qualified as a pilot in 1925, becoming one of the Navy's early aviators. During World War II he commanded two ships: the USS Suwannee and the USS Yorktown. He then commanded aircraft carrier divisions in Task Force 58 in the western Pacific Ocean. He earned 12 battle stars in the Pacific Theater and one in the Atlantic.

Finally, during the Korean War, Clark commanded Task Force 77 and later the Seventh Fleet.

Clarence "Tinq" Rogers, Prisoner of War

"Tinq" Rogers, a Cherokee, enlisted in the Army in May of 1941 at Fort Bragg, North Carolina. He was shipped to Manila, Philippine Islands, in October of that same year, as a member of the 803rd Engineers Company.

In the Philippines, Corporal Rogers was part of the team that was building roads near the Dell Carmen Airport. He was captured by the Japanese in April, 1942, after five days and nights of heavy fighting in the area.

He was one of the many American soldiers forced on the "Bataan Death March" for seven days and nights. Prisoners of war barely had anything to eat and were kept in crowded, unsanitary camps during this march.

Along with other Army engineers, Rogers was forced to work for the Japanese building roads and bridges, and then at the Caban Atican Prison Camp, was forced to perform manual labor on a farm.

In September, 1943, the Japanese moved him to the Japanese mainland where he worked in a foundry. There he was beaten and had to sleep on the floor of an unheated building. He was made to walk to work through five foot snow in straw boots and denim clothing.

In 1944, he contracted double pneumonia and was incapacitated for seven months. When he returned to the foundry, his weight dropped to 94 pounds due to a cut in the workers' rations.

When the war ended, Rogers recuperated in American Army hospitals for about seven months before he was discharged in May, 1946, at Fort Bragg.

PFC Charles George, Eastern Cherokee
Medal of Honor Recipient

Private First Class Charles George died in the Korean conflict on November 30, 1952, when he fell on a bursting grenade and smothered it to save his fellow soldiers. For this brave and selfless act, he was posthumously awarded the Congressional Medal of Honor.

He was further honored later in 1959 back in Cherokee, North Carolina, when the people of that community named their high school gymnasium after him. Private George had attended school there and had been a member of that tribe.

Sgt. John Burgess, Cherokee
Purple Heart and Numerous Decorations

Sergeant John Burgess was killed in action in Vietnam on April 19, 1969 and was posthumously awarded three medals for his valorous service. His Bronze Star citation states that Sgt. Burgess disregarded his own safety, took up an exposed position and then returned fire on enemy positions. He then moved among his unit giving instructions and encouragement to his men until he was mortally wounded by hostile fire.

He received an additional special Bronze Star with an Oak Leaf Cluster for valorous actions on April 18, 1969. That citation states: Sgt. Burgess' personal bravery and devotion to duty were in keeping with the highest traditions of the military service …"

Finally, Burgess received the Silver Star with First Oak Leaf Cluster for gallantry in action involving close combat with an armed hostile force in Vietnam. In part, the citations states: Sgt. Burgess distinguished himself by exceptionally valorous actions on February 28 and March 1, 1969, while serving as an Armored Vehicle Commander with Troop C, 3rd Squadron, 5th Cavalry, on a combat mission in Quang Tri Province … In an area where friendly forces were heavily engaged with a large enemy element, Sgt. Burgess directed his vehicle into the midst of the hostile emplacements and played a vital role in routing the enemy … When a vehicle in front of him was hit by a rocket propelled grenade, he moved his own vehicle into the line of fire to provide cover as the wounded men were evacuated.

"Sgt. Burgess' extraordinary heroism … was in keeping with the highest traditions of the military service and reflects great credit upon himself, the 9th infantry division and the U.S. Army."

Bernie Whitebear, Lakes Indian (Sin-Aikst) Army Green Beret

Indian activist Bernie Whitebear, born Bernard Reyes on the Colville Reservation in 1937, enlisted in the army in 1957 at the age of 20. He was sent to Fort Ord, California, for basic training, and then went on to Fort Campbell, Kentucky, to become a paratrooper in the 101st Airborne division.

His sense of humor and easy-going style earned Bernie many friends during his term of service. He came to enjoy jumping out of airplanes, and he carried his camera with him on jumps so he could take pictures of his army buddies floating down in their parachutes.

He went on to become a Green Beret, which called for even more intensive training, and after the end of his tour of duty in 1959, he joined an Army Reserve Special Forces team of Green Berets in South Tacoma, Washington, to continue his service.

Bernie had faced prejudice against Indians much of his life and knew firsthand of the hardships born by low income urban Indians, so on his return to civilian life, he dedicated himself to the struggle for Indian rights. In 1970, he founded the *United Indians of All Tribes Foundation*, which continues to serve the needs of the Indians of Seattle to this day. Bernie passed away in July, 2000, after a lengthy battle with cancer.[*]

*source: Reyes, Lawney, *Bernie Whitebear: An Urban Indian's Quest for Justice*. Tucson, Arizona: University of Arizona Press, 2006.

NATIVE AMERICAN WOMEN IN SERVICE

(This section is quoted verbatim with permission from the Department of Defense. The source is a DOD Web site: www.defenselink.mil/ specials/ nativeamerican01/women.htm.)

Very little is recorded or known about the contributions of Native American women to the United States military. "The Women In Military Service For America" Memorial Foundation is attempting to fill this gap by encouraging Native American women veterans to register with the Memorial so that their stories may be recorded and preserved. They are also conducting research on the contributions of Native American women of earlier eras.

Historians have only recently rediscovered and verified the actions of an Oneida woman, Tyonajanegen, at the battle of Oriskany during the American Revolution (1775–1783). As mentioned in Part Two of this book, Tyonajanegen was the wife of the Oneida war chief Hanyery. She fought at her husband's side on horseback during the battle, loading her husband's gun for him after he was shot in the wrist.

The story of Sacajawea, the Shoshone woman who accompanied the Lewis and Clark expedition of the early 19th century, is somewhat better known. Since this expedition was carried out under U.S. Army supervision and coordination, it was considered a military operation. Much of what is common knowledge about the expedition's only Indian participant is myth, however. Sacajawea has been remembered as a guide. In reality, she served as an interpreter for members of the expedition, who were unfamiliar with the Indian language. "Bird Woman's" service is described in the journals kept by Army Captains Meriwether Lewis and William Clark during the expedition.

Four Native American Catholic Sisters from Fort Berthold, South Dakota worked as nurses for the War Department during the Spanish American War (1898). Originally assigned to the military hospital at Jacksonville, Florida, the nurses were soon transferred to Havana, Cuba. One of the nurses, Sister Anthony died of disease in Cuba and was buried with military honors.

Fourteen Native American women served as members of the Army Nurse Corps during World War I, two of them overseas. Mrs. Cora E. Sinnard, a member of the Oneida Tribe and a graduate of the Episcopalian School of Nursing in Philadelphia, served eighteen months in France with a hospital unit provided by the Episcopal Church. Charlotte Edith (Anderson) Monture of the Iroquois Nation also served as an Army nurse in France. Charlotte was born in 1890 in Ohsweken, Ontario, Canada. In 1917, she left her job as an elementary school nurse to join the Army Nurse Corps. She later referred to her service in France at a military hospital as "the adventure of a lifetime." Charlotte passed away in 1996, at the age of 106.

Nearly 800 Native American women served in the military during World War II. Elva (Tapedo) Wale, a Kiowa, left her Oklahoma reservation to join the Women's Army Corps. Private Tapedo became an "Air WAC," and worked on Army Air Bases across the United States. Corporal Bernice (Firstshoot) Bailey of Lodge Pole, Montana, joined the Women's Army Corps in 1945 and served until 1948. After the war, she was sent to Wiesbaden, Germany, as part of the Army of Occupation. Beatrice (Coffey) Thayer also served in the Army of Occupation in Germany. Beatrice remembers being assigned to KP with German POWs, who were accompanied by armed guards. Beatrice was in Germany when the Berlin Wall went up, and remained in the Army until the 1970s.

Alida (Whipple) Fletcher joined the Army during World War II and trained as a medical specialist. She was assigned to the hospital at Camp Stoneman, California, which was an Army port of embarkation for the Pacific. Alida was on duty the night two ships loaded with explosives collided at a nearby ammunition dump, killing approximately 400 sailors and wounding many more. The wounded were brought to the hospital where Alida worked. She remembers that night as the most tragic of her life.

First Lieutenant Julia (Nashanany) Reeves, a member of the Potawatomie Indian Tribe of Crandon, Wisconsin, joined the Army Nurse Corps in 1942, and was assigned to one of the first medical Units shipped to the Pacific. The 52nd Evacuation Hospital Unit was sent to

New Caledonia before its members had received their Army uniforms. When the hospital ship *Solace* arrived at New Caledonia, Julia was assigned temporary duty aboard the ship. The following year, Julia was transferred to the 23rd Station Hospital in Norwich, England, where she was stationed during the invasion of Normandy. She remained in Norwich through V-J Day, returning shortly afterward to the United States. During the Korean War, Julia mobilized with the 804th Station Hospital.

Private Minnie Spotted-Wolf of Heart Butte, Montana, enlisted in the Marine Corps Women's Reserve in July 1943. She was the first female American Indian to enroll in the Corps. Minnie had worked on her father's ranch doing such chores as cutting fence posts, driving a two-ton truck, and breaking horses. Her comment on Marine boot camp "Hard but not too hard."

Ola Mildred Rexroat, an Oglala Sioux from Pine Ridge Indian Reservation, South Dakota, joined the Women's Airforce Service Pilots (WASP) directly out of high school. Her job was to tow targets for aerial gunnery students at Eagle Pass Army Air Base in Texas. Towing targets for student gunners was a fairly dangerous assignment, but "Rexy" was happy to be able to contribute to the war effort in a meaningful way. After the war ended, Ola joined the Air Force and served for almost ten years.

During the 1950s and 1960s, fewer women felt the call to military service (*reason unknown*). The services, however, were in desperate need of womanpower during the Korean conflict and the Vietnam War, and conducted extensive recruitment campaigns aimed at young women. Many Native American women answered their country's call. Sarah Mae Peshlakai, a member of the Navajo Tribe from Crystal, New Mexico, enlisted in the Women's Army Corps in 1951 and served until 1957. Peshlakai trained as a medical specialist and was assigned to Yokohama Army Hospital in Japan, where she helped care for casualties from the Korean battlefields.

Verna Fender entered the Navy during the Korean Conflict and trained at Bainbridge, Maryland. She was severely injured during basic training and was sent to a Navy hospital for physical rehabilitation. Undeterred, Verna returned to Bainbridge and completed her training. The Navy assigned Verna to its base in San Diego, California, where she completed her 3-year term of enlistment, working in the departments of berthing and sectioning, supply, and ordnance. Shirley M. Arviso, a Navajo of the Bitter Water Clan, served in the Navy from 1953 through 1963. She was the Communications Officer in charge of a group of people who decrypted classified messages.

Pearl Ross, a member of the Arikara Tribe from the Fort Berthold Reservation, joined the Air Force in 1953, and trained as a medical specialist. Her first assignment was to the Air Force hospital in Cheyenne, Wyoming. Pearl was then assigned to Offutt Air Force Base in Nebraska, where she worked in the 865th Medical Group at SAC HQ. During the Vietnam era, she saw many men who had been wounded in the combat theater. Pearl volunteered for overseas duty, but was turned down because the Air Force was hesitant to send women to Vietnam.

Linda Woods enlisted in the Air Force in the late 1950s and was on duty when President Kennedy was assassinated. She remembers that the air base where she was stationed went on full alert. A later assignment took her to the southern United States during the Civil Rights movement. As a non-white, she found the environment somewhat difficult; however, she retained pride in her uniform as a woman of color.

Barbara Monteiro joined the WAC in 1963 and took her basic and secretarial training at Ft. McClellan, Alabama. Her first duty assignment was to Ft. Huachuca, Arizona, where she worked for three years in the travel office and motor pool in support of troop readiness during the Vietnam War. In 1966, Monteiro was assigned to Ft. Richardson, Alaska, where she served as an administration specialist at the Education Center for a year. Lance Corporal Valla Dee Jack Egge of Dougherty, Oklahoma, served in the U.S. Marine Corps in the early 1960s as the executive secretary to two commanding generals of the Parris Island Marine Corps Base, South Carolina.

Increasing numbers of women, including Native Americans, entered the military in the 1970s and 1980s. Patricia White Bear joined the Navy in 1981. She trained as an Instrumentman and served at sea repairing, adjusting and calibrating the wide variety of mechanical measuring instruments used aboard ships. Dolores Kathleen Smith, a Cherokee, graduated from the Air Force Academy in 1982. She completed navigator training and was assigned to a KC-135 unit. She served in the operational plans division of her unit and also as an instructor before retiring as a captain from the Air Force in 1990.

Darlene Yellowcloud of the Lakota Tribe was inspired to join the Army because so many of the men in her family had served. Her grandfather, Bear Saves Life, was killed in action in France during World War I. Her father, brothers, brothers-in-law, uncles and cousins were all veterans. Darlene was assigned to the U. S. Army in Korea as a Specialist 4th Class. Lawnikwa Spotted-Eaglefortune joined the Army in 1988, and attended Basic Training at Fort Dix, New Jersey. Acting as a guide-on carrier, she was injured when another carrier grounded a guide iron through her foot into the ground. She still has the scar, and now serves as a member of the Virginia Air National Guard.

As of 1980, at least sixty Native American women were serving in the Eskimo Scouts, a special unit of the Alaska National Guard. The Eskimo Scouts patrol the western coastline of Alaska and the islands separating Alaska and Russia. The Scouts are the only members of the National Guard who have a continuous active duty mission. This unit was organized during World War II, and the wives of scout battalion members have always been involved in patrol missions. Women were admitted as official members in 1976, and only then began to receive pay, benefits and recognition for their work. Scouts currently patrol ice flows in the Bering Straits, monitor movements on the tundra, and perform Arctic search and rescue efforts as required.

Native American women lost their lives while in the service of their nation. Katherine Matthews of Cherokee, North Carolina, joined the Navy in the late 1970s and trained as an Aviation Machinist's Mate. She died while serving in California in 1985. Terri Ann Hagen, a former Army medic, was a member of the Army National Guard when she was killed fighting a fire on Storm King Mountain in Colorado in 1994.

APPENDIX II
The Record of Service

CHART OF NATIVE AMERICAN MILITARY SERVICE

World War I	8,000 served in the Army
	6,000 served in the Navy
World War II	25,000 served. Awards included:
	71 Air medals, 51 Silver Stars,
	47 Bronze Stars,
	34 Distinguished Flying Crosses,
	2 Congressional Medals of Honor
Korean Conflict	Unknown number served
	1 Congressional Medal of Honor
Vietnam era	41,500
Desert Storm era	24,000 (3,000 deployed in Kuwait)
Iraq War era	17,500

Source: U.S. Dept. of Interior, Bureau of Indian Affairs

Serving Today:
According to DOD records, approximately 18,000 Native Americans serve in all branches of the U.S. military today.*

*Source: Office of Public Affairs, Department of Defense, the Pentagon, Washington DC

NATIVE AMERICAN RECIPIENTS OF THE CONGRESSIONAL MEDAL OF HONOR

*Source: All information in this section is taken verbatim from www.army. mil/CHM-pg/topics/natam/natam-moh.html and is used with permission from the Pentagon Public Affairs Office. (Note: these records are part of the U.S. public domain.)

The Indian War Period

ALCHESAY—Rank and organization: Sergeant, Indian Scouts. Place and date: Winter of 1872–73. Entered service at: Camp Verde, Ariz. Born: 1853, Arizona Territory. Date of issue: 12 April 1875. Citation: Gallant conduct during campaigns and engagements with Apaches.

BLANQUET—Rank and organization: Indian Scouts. Place and date: Winter of 1872–73. Birth: Arizona. Date of issue: 12 April 1875. Citation: Gallant conduct during campaigns and engagements with Apaches.

CHIQUITO—Rank and organization: Indian Scouts. Place and date: Winter of 1871–73. Birth: Arizona. Date of issue: 12 April 1875. Citation: Gallant conduct during campaigns and engagements with Apaches.

CO-RUX-TE-CHOD-ISH (Mad Bear)—Rank and organization: Sergeant, Pawnee Scouts, U.S. Army. Place and date: At Republican River, Kans., 8 July 1869. Birth: Nebraska. Date of issue: 24 August 1869. Citation: Ran out from the command in pursuit of a dismounted Indian; was shot down and badly wounded by a bullet from his own command.

ELSATSOOSU—Rank and organization: Corporal, Indian Scouts. Place and date: Winter of 1872–73. Birth: Arizona. Date of issue: 12 April 1875. Citation: Gallant conduct during campaigns and engagements with Apaches.

FACTOR, POMPEY—Rank and organization: Private, Indian Scouts. Place and date: At Pecos River, Tex., 25 April 1875. Birth: Arkansas. Date of issue: 28 May 1875. Citation: With 3 other men, he participated in a charge against 25 hostiles while on a scouting patrol.

JIM—Rank and organization: Sergeant, Indian Scouts. Place and date: Winter of 1871–73. Birth: Arizona Territory. Date of issue: 12 April 1875. Citation: Gallant conduct during campaigns and engagements with Apaches.

KELSAY—Rank and organization: Indian Scouts. Place and date: Winter of 1872–73. Birth: Arizona. Date of issue: 12 April 1875. Citation: Gallant conduct during campaigns and engagements with Apaches.

KOSOHA—Rank and organization: Indian Scouts. Place and date: Winter of 1872–73. Birth: Arizona. Date of issue: 12 April 1875. Citation: Gallant conduct during campaigns and engagements with Apaches.

MACHOL—Rank and organization: Private, Indian Scouts. Place and date: Arizona, 1872–73. Birth: Arizona. Date of issue: 12 April 1875. Citation: Gallant conduct during campaign and engagements with Apaches.

NANNASADDIE—Rank and organization: Indian Scouts. Place and date: 1872–73. Birth: Arizona. Date of issue: 12 April 1875. Citation: Gallant conduct during campaigns and engagements with Apaches.

NANTAJE (NANTAHE)—Rank and organization: Indian Scouts. Place and date: 1872–73. Birth: Arizona. Date of issue: 12 April 1875. Citation: Gallant conduct during campaigns and engagements with Apaches.

PAINE, ADAM—Rank and organization: Private, Indian Scouts. Place and date: Canyon Blanco tributary of the Red River, Tex., 26–27 September 1874. Entered service at: Fort Duncan, Texas. Birth: Florida.

Date of issue: 13 October 1875. Citation: Rendered invaluable service to Col. R. S. Mackenzie, 4th U.S. Cavalry, during this engagement.

PAYNE, ISAAC—Rank and organization: Trumpeter, Indian Scouts. Place and date: At Pecos River, Tex., 25 April 1875. Birth: Mexico. Date of issue: 28 May 1875. Citation: With 3 other men, he participated in a charge against 25 hostiles while on a scouting patrol.

ROWDY—Rank and organization: Sergeant, Company A, Indian Scouts. Place and date: Arizona, 7 March 1890. Birth: Arizona. Date of issue: 15 May 1890. Citation: Bravery in action with Apache Indians.

WARD, JOHN—Rank and organization: Sergeant, 24th U.S. Infantry Indian Scouts Place and date: At Pecos River, Tex., 25 April 1875. Entered service at. Fort Duncan, Tex. Birth: Arkansas. Date of issue: 28 May 1875. Citation. With 3 other men, he participated in a charge against 25 hostiles while on a scouting patrol.

World War II

BARFOOT, VAN T.—Rank and organization: Second Lieutenant, U.S. Army, 157th Infantry, 45th Infantry Division. Place and date: Near Carano, Italy, 23 May 1944. Entered service at: Carthage, Miss. Birth: Edinburg, Miss. G.O. No.: 79, 4 October 1944. Citation: For conspicuous gallantry and intrepidity at the risk of life above and beyond the call of duty on 23 May 1944, near Carano, Italy. With his platoon heavily engaged during an assault against forces well entrenched on commanding ground, 2d Lt. Barfoot (then Tech. Sgt.) moved off alone upon the enemy left flank. He crawled to the proximity of 1 machinegun nest and made a direct hit on it with a hand grenade, killing 2 and wounding 3 Germans. He continued along the German defense line to another machinegun emplacement, and with his tommygun killed 2 and captured 3 soldiers. Members of another enemy machinegun crew then abandoned their position and gave themselves up to Sgt. Barfoot. Leaving the prisoners for his support squad to pick up, he proceeded to mop up positions in the immediate area, capturing more prisoners and bringing his total count to 17. Later that day, after he had reorganized his men and consolidated the newly captured ground, the enemy launched a fierce armored counterattack directly at his platoon positions. Securing a bazooka, Sgt. Barfoot took up an exposed position directly in front of 3 advancing Mark VI tanks. From a distance of 75 yards his first shot destroyed the track of the leading tank, effectively disabling it, while the other 2 changed direction toward the flank. As the crew of the disabled tank dismounted, Sgt. Barfoot killed 3 of them with his tommygun. He continued onward into enemy terrain and destroyed a recently abandoned German fieldpiece with a demolition charge placed in the breech. While returning to his platoon position, Sgt. Barfoot, though greatly fatigued by his Herculean efforts, assisted 2 of his seriously wounded men 1,700 yards to a position of safety. Sgt. Barfoot's extraordinary heroism, demonstration of magnificent valor, and aggressive determination in the face of pointblank fire are a perpetual inspiration to his fellow soldiers.

CHILDERS, ERNEST—Rank and organization: Second Lieutenant, U.S. Army, 45th Infantry Division. Place and date: At Oliveto, Italy, 22 September 1943. Entered service at: Tulsa, Okla. Birth: Broken Arrow, Okla. G.O. No.: 30, 8 April 1944. Citation: For conspicuous gallantry and intrepidity at risk of life above and beyond the call of duty in action on 22 September 1943, at Oliveto, Italy. Although 2d Lt. Childers previously had just suffered a fractured instep he, with 8 enlisted men, advanced up a hill toward enemy machinegun nests. The group advanced to a rock wall overlooking a cornfield and 2d Lt. Childers ordered a base of fire laid across the field so that he could advance. When he was fired upon by 2 enemy snipers from a nearby house he killed both of them. He moved behind the machinegun nests and killed all occupants of the nearer one. He continued toward the second one and threw rocks into it. When the 2 occupants of the nest raised up, he shot 1. The other was killed by 1 of the 8 enlisted men. 2d Lt. Childers continued his advance toward a house farther up the hill, and single-handed, captured an enemy mortar observer. The exceptional leadership, initiative, calmness under fire, and conspicuous gallantry displayed by 2d Lt. Childers were an inspiration to his men.

EVANS, ERNEST EDWIN—Rank and organization: Commander, U.S. Navy. Born: 13 August 1908, Pawnee, Okla. Accredited to: Oklahoma. Other Navy awards: Navy Cross, Bronze Star Medal. Citation: For conspicuous gallantry and intrepidity at the risk of his life above and beyond the call of duty as commanding officer of the U.S.S. Johnston in action against major units of the enemy Japanese fleet during the battle off Samar on 25 October 1944. The first to lay a smokescreen and to open fire as an enemy task force, vastly superior in number, firepower and armor, rapidly approached. Comdr. Evans gallantly diverted the powerful blasts of hostile guns from the lightly armed and armored carriers under his protection, launching the first torpedo attack when the Johnston came under straddling Japanese shellfire. Undaunted by damage sustained under the terrific volume of fire, he unhesitatingly joined others of his group to provide fire support during subsequent torpedo attacks against the Japanese and, outshooting and outmaneuvering the enemy as he consistently interposed his vessel between the hostile fleet units and our carriers despite the crippling loss of engine power and communications with steering aft, shifted command to the fantail, shouted steering orders through an open hatch to men turning the rudder by hand and battled furiously until the Johnston, burning and shuddering from a mortal blow, lay dead in the water after 3 hours of fierce combat. Seriously wounded early in the engagement, Comdr. Evans, by his indomitable courage and brilliant professional skill, aided materially in turning back the enemy during a critical phase of the action. His valiant fighting spirit throughout this historic battle will venture as an inspiration to all who served with him.

MONTGOMERY, JACK C.—Rank and organization: First Lieutenant, U.S. Army, 45th Infantry Division. Place and date: Near, Padiglione, Italy, 22 February 1944. Entered service at: Sallisaw, Okla. Birth: Long, Okla. G.O. No.: 5, 15 January 1945. Citation: For conspicuous gallantry and intrepidity at risk of life above and beyond the call of duty on 22 February 1944, near Padiglione, Italy. Two hours before daybreak a strong force of enemy infantry established themselves in 3 echelons at 50 yards, 100 yards, and 300 yards, respectively, in front of the rifle platoons commanded by 1st Lt. Montgomery. The closest position, consisting of 4 machineguns and 1 mortar, threatened the immediate security of the platoon position. Seizing an Ml rifle and several hand grenades, 1st Lt. Montgomery crawled up a ditch to within hand grenade range of the enemy. Then climbing boldly onto a little mound, he fired his rifle and threw his grenades so accurately that he killed 8 of the enemy and captured the remaining 4. Returning to his platoon, he called for artillery fire on a house, in and around which he suspected that the majority of the enemy had entrenched themselves. Arming himself with a carbine, he proceeded along the shallow ditch, as withering fire from the riflemen and machine gunners in the second position was concentrated on him. He attacked this position with such fury that 7 of the enemy surrendered to him, and both machineguns were silenced. Three German dead were found in the vicinity later that morning. 1st Lt. Montgomery continued boldly toward the house, 300 yards from his platoon position. It was now daylight, and the enemy observation was excellent across the flat open terrain which led to 1st Lt. Montgomery's objective. When the artillery barrage had lifted, 1st Lt. Montgomery ran fearlessly toward the strongly defended position. As the enemy started streaming out of the house, 1st Lt. Montgomery, unafraid of treacherous snipers, exposed himself daringly to assemble the surrendering enemy and send them to the rear. His fearless, aggressive, and intrepid actions that morning, accounted for a total of 11 enemy dead, 32 prisoners, and an unknown number of wounded. That night, while aiding an adjacent unit to repulse a counterattack, he was struck by mortar fragments and seriously wounded. The selflessness and courage exhibited by 1st Lt. Montgomery in alone attacking 3 strong enemy positions inspired his men to a degree beyond estimation.

REESE, JOHN N., JR.—Rank and organization: Private First Class, U.S. Army, Company B, 148th Infantry, 37th Infantry Division. Place and date: Paco Railroad Station, Manila, Philippine Islands. 9 February 1945. Entered service at: Pryor, Okla. Birth: Muskogee, Okla. G.O. No.: 89, 19 October 1945. Citation. He was engaged in the attack on the Paco Railroad Station, which was strongly defended by 300 determined enemy soldiers with machineguns and rifles, supported by several pillboxes, 3 20mm. guns, 1 37-mm. gun and heavy mortars. While making a frontal assault across an open field, his platoon was halted 100 yards from the station by intense enemy fire. On his own initiative he left the platoon accompanied by a comrade, and continued forward to a house 60 yards from the objective. Although under constant enemy observation, the 2 men remained in this position for an hour, firing at targets of opportunity, killing more than 35 Japanese and wounding many more. Moving closer to the station and discovering a group of Japanese replacements attempting to reach pillboxes, they opened heavy fire, killed more than 40 and stopped all subsequent attempts to man the emplacements. Enemy fire became more intense as they advanced to within 20 yards of the station. From that point Pfc. Reese provided effective covering fire and courageously drew enemy fire to himself while his companion killed 7 Japanese and destroyed a 20-mm. gun and heavy machinegun with hand grenades. With their ammunition running low, the 2 men started to return to the American lines, alternately providing covering fire for each other as they withdrew. During this movement, Pfc. Reese was killed by enemy fire as he reloaded his rifle. The intrepid team, in 21/2 hours of fierce fighting, killed more than 82 Japanese, completely disorganized their defense and paved the way for subsequent complete defeat of the enemy at this strong point. By his gallant determination in the face of tremendous odds, aggressive fighting spirit, and extreme heroism at the cost of his life, Pfc. Reese materially aided the advance of our troops in Manila and providing a lasting inspiration to all those with whom he served.

Korean War

GEORGE, CHARLES—Rank and organization: Private First Class, U.S. Army, Company C, 179th Infantry Regiment, 45th Infantry Division. Place and date: Near Songnae-dong, Korea, 30 November 1952. Entered service at: Whittier, N.C. Born: 23 August 1932, Cherokee, N.C. G.O. NO.: 19, 18 March 1954. Citation: Pfc. George, a member of Company C, distinguished himself by conspicuous gallantry and outstanding courage above and beyond the call of duty in action against the enemy on the night of 30 November 1952. He was a member of a raiding party committed to engage the enemy and capture a prisoner for interrogation. Forging up the rugged slope of the key terrain feature, the group was subjected to intense mortar and machine gun fire and suffered several casualties. Throughout the advance, he fought valiantly and, upon reaching the crest of the hill, leaped into the trenches and closed with the enemy in hand-to-hand combat. When friendly troops were ordered to move back upon completion of the assignment, he and 2 comrades remained to cover the withdrawal. While in the process of leaving the trenches, a hostile soldier hurled a grenade into their midst. Pfc. George shouted a warning to 1 comrade, pushed the other soldier out of danger, and, with full knowledge of the consequences, unhesitatingly threw himself upon the grenade, absorbing the full blast of the explosion. Although seriously wounded in this display of valor, he refrained from any outcry which would divulge the position of his companions. The 2 soldiers evacuated him to the forward aid station and shortly thereafter he succumbed to his wound. Pfc. George's indomitable courage, consummate devotion to duty, and willing self-sacrifice reflect the highest credit upon himself and uphold the finest traditions of the military service.

HARVEY, RAYMOND—Rank and organization: Captain, U.S. Army, Company C, 17th Infantry Regiment. Place and date: Vicinity of Taemi-Dong, Korea, 9 March 1951. Entered service at: Pasadena, Calif. Born: 1 March 1920 Ford City, Pa. G.O. No.: 67, 2 August 1951. Citation: Capt. Harvey Company C, distinguished himself by conspicuous gallantry and intrepidity above and beyond the call of duty in action. When his company was pinned down by a barrage of automatic weapons fire from numerous well-entrenched emplacements, imperiling accomplishment of its mission, Capt. Harvey braved a hail of fire and exploding grenades to advance to the first enemy machine gun nest, killing its crew with grenades. Rushing to the edge of the next emplacement, he killed its crew with carbine fire. He then moved the 1st Platoon forward until it was again halted by a curtain of automatic fire from well fortified hostile positions. Disregarding the hail of fire, he personally charged and neutralized a third emplacement. Miraculously escaping death from intense crossfire, Capt. Harvey continued to lead the assault. Spotting an enemy pillbox well camouflaged by logs, he moved close enough to sweep the emplacement with carbine fire and throw grenades through the openings, annihilating its 5 occupants. Though wounded he then turned to order the company forward, and, suffering agonizing pain, he continued to direct the reduction of the remaining hostile positions, refusing evacuation until assured that the mission would be accomplished. Capt. Harvey's valorous and intrepid actions served as an inspiration to his company, reflecting the utmost glory upon himself and upholding the heroic traditions of the military service.

RED CLOUD, MITCHELL, JR.—Rank and organization: Corporal, U S. Army, Company E, 19th Infantry Regiment, 24th Infantry Division. Place and date: Near Chonghyon, Korea, 5 November 1950. Entered service at: Merrilan Wis. Born: 2 July 1924, Hatfield, Wis. G.O. No.: 26, 25 April 1951. Citation: Cpl. Red Cloud, Company E, distinguished himself by conspicuous gallantry and intrepidity above and beyond the call of duty in action against the enemy. From his position on the point of a ridge immediately in front of the company command post he was the first to detect the approach of the Chinese Communist forces and give the alarm as the enemy charged from a brush-covered area less than 100 feet from him. Springing up he delivered devastating pointblank automatic rifle fire into the advancing enemy. His accurate and intense fire checked this assault and gained time for the company to consolidate its defense. With utter fearlessness he maintained his firing position until severely wounded by enemy fire. Refusing assistance he pulled himself to his feet and wrapping his arm around a tree continued his deadly fire again, until he was fatally wounded. This heroic act stopped the enemy from overrunning his company's position and gained time for reorganization and evacuation of the wounded. Cpl. Red Cloud's dauntless courage and gallant self-sacrifice reflects the highest credit upon himself and upholds the esteemed traditions of the U.S. Army.

SOURCES:
Citations, Interviewees, Bibliography, and Archives

Citations

Part One

1. Starkey, Armstrong. *European and Native American Warfare, 1675–1815*. Norman, OK: University of Oklahoma Press, 1998.

2. Weatherford, Jack. *Native Roots*. NY, NY: Crown Publishers, 1991.

3. Truman, Harry S. "America's Treatment of the Indians." Independence, MO: Presidential papers of the Harry S. Truman Library (public domain).

4. Brown, Dee. *Bury My Heart at Wounded Knee*. NY, NY: Holt, Rinehart and Winston, NY, 1971.

Part Two

1. Johansen, Bruce. *Forgotten Founders: The Iroquois and the Rationale for the American Revolution*. Ipswich, MA: Gambit, Inc. Publishers, 1982.

2. *Pennsylvania Journal & Weekly Advertiser*. Philadelphia, PA. Sept. 3, 1777.

3. Waldo, Albgence. *The Diary of Dr. Albigence Waldo*. Washington DC: National Archives, American Revolutionary War Papers, 1777.

4. Nabokov, Peter, ed. *Native American Testimony*. NY, NY: Viking Penguin, 1991.

5. "The Battle at Pea Ridge," *New York Illustrated News*. NY, NY: April 12, 1862.

6. Ambrose, Stephen E., ed. *A Wisconsin Boy in Dixie: Civil War Letters of James K. Newton*. Madison, WI: University of Wisconsin Press, 1961.

7. Union and Confederate War Department Papers, National Archives, Washington DC.

8. Armstrong, William H. *Warrior in Two Camps: Ely Parker.* Syracuse, NY: Syracuse University Press, 1978.

9. Ibid.

10. Act of Congress, July 28, 1866; National Archives, Washington DC.

11. National Archives, Washington DC.

12. Glass, Laurence C. "A Short History of the Indians in the U.S. Military" (unpublished manuscript), 1982.

13. Downey, Fairfax and Jacobsen, Jacques Noel, Jr. *The Red/Bluecoats: The Indian Scouts, U.S. Army.* Ft. Collins, CO: Old Army Press, 1973.

14. Dunlay, Thomas W. *Wolves for the Blue Soldiers: Indian Scouts and Auxiliaries with the US Army 1860–1890.* Lincoln, NE: Univ. of Nebraska Press, 1982.

15. Brown, Dee. *Bury My Heart at Wounded Knee.* NY, NY: Holt, Rinehart and Winston, 1971.

16. *New York Times,* December 27, 1893.

17. Roosevelt, Theodore. *The Rough Riders.* NY, NY: Charles Scribner and Sons, 1899.

Part Three

1. "Transmitting Messages in Choctaw," Report to Captain Spence, Commanding General, 36th Division, Washington DC, January 23, 1919. U.S. Military Archives.

2. "Germans Confused by Choctaw Code Talkers," *Bishinik* (Choctaw Tribal Newspaper). August, 1986.

3. "France to Honor Choctaw Code Talkers," *Bishinik.* October, 1989.

4. Bureau of Indian Affairs, Records Group 75, National Archives, Seattle Branch.

5. "Code Talkers Recognition Act"—proposed congressional legislation introduced several different times by different senators/representatives but never passed into law.

6. Robinson, Gary. *A Time to Heal.* Documentary short film, 1988.

7. Ibid.

8. Ibid.

9. *Indian Country Today* (newspaper) online archives.

10. Ibid.

11. Davidson, Osha Gray. "A Wrong Turn in the Desert," *Rolling Stone.* May 27, 2004.

Part Four

1. Keen, Sam. *Faces of the Enemy.* NY, NY: Harper Collins, reprint edition, 1991.

2. Ferguson, R. Brian. "Tribal Warfare," *Scientific American*, 1992: pp. 108–113.

3. Riley, Glenda. *Women and Indians on the Frontier, 1825–1915.* Albuquerque, NM: University of New Mexico Press, 1984.

4. National Archives, Washington DC.

Part Five

1. Primary Source: "Native Americans and the Military: Today and Yesterday," published by the U.S. Army Public Affairs Information Branch, March, 1984.

2. Department of Defense Web site: www.defenselink.mil/specials/nativeamerican01/women.htm.

Contemporary Witnesses/Interviewees*

(presented alphabetically)
George Amiotte (Lakota), Vietnam Veteran
Mary Anderson (Pima), Quoted from Lakota Times
Apesanahkwat (Menominee), Vietnam Veteran
Harold Barse, Vietnam Era Veterans Inter-Tribal Association
Alison Bernstein, Author, *American Indians and World War II*
Mike Berryhill (Creek), Vietnam Veteran
Schlict Billy (Choctaw), WWII Codetalker—European Theater
Dee Brown, Author, *Bury My Heart at Wounded Knee*
Charles Chibitty (Comanche), WWII Veteran
Amos Christjohn (Oneida), WWII Veteran
Erwin Christjohn (Oneida), Korean Veteran
Ted Christjohn (Oneida), Vietnam Veteran
R. Brian Ferguson, Author/Professor
Harold Foster (Navajo), WWII Codetalker
Carl Gorman (Navajo), WWII Codetalker
Paul Greenberg, Newspaper Columnist
Duane Hale, PhD (Creek), Historian/Professor
Nathan Hart (S. Cheyenne), Former Director, Oklahoma Indian Affairs Commission
Tom Holm, PhD (Cherokee), Vietnam Veteran/Professor
Sam Keen, Author, *Faces of the Enemy*
Laura Larkin (Oneida)
Eddie Little Light (Crow), Vietnam Veteran
Douglas Long (Wisconsin Winnebago), Korean Veteran
Jan Malcolm (Oneida), Vietnam Veteran, Oneida Museum Director
Joe Medicine Crow (Crow), WWII Veteran/Tribal Historian
Barney Old Coyote, PhD (Crow), WWII Veteran, Historian/Professor
Alfonso Ortiz (San Juan Pueblo), Anthropologist/Author (deceased)
Alice Petrivelli (Aleut)
Ministri Philemonof (Aleut)
Carol Red Cherries (N. Cheyenne), Army Veteran/Tribal Supreme Court Judge

Windy Shoulderblade (N. Cheyenne), Vietnam Veteran
Sherry L. Smith (N. Cheyenne), U.T.E.P.
John Stands-In-Timber (Cheyenne), Author/Historian
Ronald Stewart (Crow), Korean War Veteran
William Charles Stewart (Crow), Korean War Veteran
Joe Walks-Along (N. Cheyenne), WWII Veteran
Carson Walks-Over-The-Ice (Crow), Vietnam Veteran
Jack Weatherford, Author/Anthropologist, *Indian Givers*
Ruth Williams (Navajo), Desert Storm Veteran
Russell Winfield (N. Cheyenne), Vietnam Veteran/Tribal Police Officer

*All interviews were conducted in the early 1990s by the authors.

Bibliography and Suggested Reading: Books and Articles

General Sources: Indians/Military History

1. Prucha, Paul. *A Bibliographical Guide to the History of Indian-White Relations in the United States.* Chicago, IL: Newberry Library, University of Chicago, 1977.

2. Hirschfelder, Arlene and Byler, Mary and Dorris, Michael. *Guide To Research On North American Indians.* Chicago, IL: American Library Association, Chicago, 1983.

3. Glass, Laurence C. "A Short History of The Indians in The U.S. Military" (unpublished article), 1982.

4. *Native Americans and the Military: Today and Yesterday,* U.S. Army Command Information Branch, Ft. McPherson, GA, March, 1984, SP 3–84.

5. Hill, Edward, ed. *Guide To The Records In The National Archives of The U.S. Relating To American Indians.* Washington DC: NARA, 1981.

6. Freeman, John F., ed. *A Guide To Manuscripts Relating To The American Indian In The Library of The American Philosophical Society.* Independence Square, Philadelphia: Amer. Philosophical Society, 1966.

7. *American Indians Today, Answers To Your Questions,* BIA: Washington, DC, 1991.

8. Lang, Walt. *United States Military Almanac.* NY, NY: Military Press/Crown Publishers, 1989.

9. Heller, Jonathan, ed. *War and Conflict: Selected Images from the National Archives, 1765–1970.* Washington DC: NARA, 1990.

Warfare: Psychology/Nature of War, etc.

1. Holmes, Richard. *Acts of War—The Behavior of Men In Battle.* NY, NY: The Free Press/Simon & Schuster, 1989.

2. Dyer, Gwynne. *War: The Lethal Custom.* NY, NY: Carroll and Graf Publishers, 2005.

3. Keen, Sam. *Faces of the Enemy.* NY, NY: Harper Collins, 1991.

4. Hass, Jonathan, ed. *The Anthropology of War.* Cambridge, MA: Cambridge University Press, 1990.

Indian Warfare

1. Wellman, Paul. *Indian Wars and Warriors East.* Boston, MA: Houghton Mifflin Co., 1959.

2. Wood, Nancy C. *War Cry on a Prayer Feather.* NY, NY: Doubleday, 1979.

3. LaFlesche, Francis. *War Ceremony and Peace Ceremony of the Osage Indians.* Washington DC: U.S. Government Printing Office, 1939.

4. Hofsinde, Robert. *Indian Warriors and Their Weapons.* NY, NY: William Morrow and Company, 1965.

5. Mails, Thomas E. *Dog Soldiers, Bear Men and Buffalo Women, A Study of the Societies and Cults of the Plains Indians.* Rutledge, NJ: Prentice-Hall, 1973.

6. Taylor, Colin. *The Warriors of the Plains.* London, England: Hamlyn Publishing Group, 1975.

7. Worcester, D. E. "The Weapons of American Indians," *New Mexico Historical Review* 20, July, 1945: pp. 227–238.

8. Cooke, David C. *Fighting Indians of America.* NY, NY: Donald Mead, 1966.

9. Mishkin, Bernard. *Rank and Warfare Among Plains Indians.* Seattle, WA: University of Washington Press, 1966.

10. Forbes, Jack D. *Warriors of the Colorado.* Norman, OK: O.U. Press, 1965.

11. Johnson, Dorothy M. *Warrior for a Lost Nation: Biography of Sitting Bull.* Philadelphia, PA: Westminster Press, 1969.

12. Ferguson, R. Brian. "Tribal Warfare," *Scientific American.* January, 1992: pp. 108–113.

13. "Militarization and Indigenous Peoples, Parts I & II" *Cultural Survival Quarterly,* Vol. 11, Nos. 3 & 4, 1987.

14. Weatherford, Jack. *Native Roots.* NY, NY: Crown Publishers, 1991.

15. Blanchard, Kendall. *The Mississippi Choctaws at Play.* Urbana, IL: University of Illinois Press, 1981.

Colonial Era

1. Malone, Patrick M. "Changing Military Technology among the Indians of the Southern New England, 1600–1677," *American Quarterly* 25, March, 1973: pp. 48–63.

2. Mahone, John K. "Anglo-American Methods of Indian Warfare, 1676–1794," *Mississippi Valley Historical Review* 45, September, 1958: pp. 254–275.

3. Mahone, John K. *Indian and English Military Systems in New England in the 17th Century.* Providence, RI: Brown University, 1971.

4. Cwiklik, Robert. *King Philip and the War with the Colonists.* Englewood Cliffs, NJ: Silver Burdett Press, 1989.

5. Smoyer, Stanley C. "Indians as Allies in the Inter-colonial Wars," *New York History* 17, Oct. 1936: p.411–22.

6. Lincoln, Charles. *Narratives of the Indian Wars, 1675–1699.* New York: Charles Scribner's Sons, 1913.

7. Penhallow, Samuel. *The History of the Wars of New England with the Eastern Indians* (1700–1725) Philadelphia, PA: Oscar H. Harpel, 1859.

Revolutionary War

1. O'Donnel III, James H. *Southern Indians in the American Revolution.* Knoxville, TN: University of Tennessee Press, 1973.

2. Shaw, Helen L. *British Administration of the Southern Indians* (Unpublished manuscript). Library of Congress, 1931.

3. Mohr, Walter. *Federal Indian Relations 1774–1788* (Unpublished manuscript). Library of Congress, 1933.

4. Washington, George. "Washington's Valley Forge Papers" (Unpublished manuscript). U.S. Army Archives: Washington DC, 1778.

5. Sullivan, Thomas. *Journal of the Operations of the American War* (Unpublished manuscript). Library of the American Philosophical Society: Philadelphia, PA, 1778.

6. Abler, Thomas S., ed. *Chainbreaker: The Revolutionary War Memoirs of Governor Blacksnake.* Lincoln, NE: University of Nebraska Press, 1989.

7. Stone, William. *Life of Joseph Brant.* NY: George Dearborn and Co., 1838.

Civil War

1. Abel, Annie Heloise. *The American Indian as Participant in the Civil War.* Lincoln, NE: University of Nebraska Press, 1992.

2. Rampp, Larry C. and Donald L. *The Civil War in the Indian Territory.* Austin, TX: Presidial Press, 1975.

3. "Civil War Reports" (Unpublished manuscript). U.S. Army Archives: Washington DC, 1865.

4. Baird, David, ed. *A Creek Warrior for the Confederacy—The Autobiography of Chief G. W. Grayson.* Norman, OK: University of Oklahoma Press, 1988.

5. Franks, Kenneth A. *Stand Watie.* Memphis, TN: Memphis State University, 1979.

6. Brown, Dee A. *The Galvanized Yankees.* Urbana, IL: University of Illinois Press, 1963.

7. Armstrong, William H. *Warrior in Two Camps: Ely S. Parker, Union General and Seneca Chief.* Syracuse, NY: Syracuse University Press, 1978.

Indian Wars (1800s)

1. Downey, Fairfax. *Indian Wars of the U.S. Army, 1776–1865.* Garden City, NY: Doubleday and Co., 1963.

2. Dillon, Richard H. *North American Indian Wars.* London, England: Magna Books, 1994.

3. Marshall, S.L.A. *Crimsoned Prairie.* NY: Scribner, 1972.

4. Schmitt, Martin H. and Dee Brown. *Fighting Indians of the West.* NY: Bonanza Books, 1948.

5. Prucha, Francis P. *A Guide to Military Posts of the United States, 1789–1895.* Madison, WI: U.S. National Park Service, 1964.

6. Wheeler, Col. Homer W. *Buffalo Days (40 Years in the Old West).* Indianapolis, IN: Bobs-Merrill Co., 1925.

7. Rickey Don. *Forty Miles a Day on Beans and Hay.* Norman, OK: University of Oklahoma Press, 1963.

8. Utley, Robert M. *Frontier Regulars: The U.S. Army and the Indian (1866–1891).* NY: MacMillan Pub. Co., 1973.

9. Longstreet, Stephen. *War Cries on Horseback (1815–1875).* London, England: W.H. Allen, 1970.

10. *Wildlife on the Plains and the Horrors of Indian Warfare.* Facsimile edition of the original work published in 1891. Arno Press, 1969

11. Riley, Glenda. *Women and Indians on the Frontier, 1825–1915.* Albuquerque, NM: University of New Mexico Press, 1984.

12. Tillet, Leslie. *Wind on the Buffalo Grass: An Indian account of the Battle of the Little Big Horn*. NY: Thomas Y. Crowell, 1976.

13. Wiltsey, Norman B. *Brave Warriors*. Caldwell, Idaho: Caxton Printers, 1963.

14. Brandes, Raymond, ed. *Troopers West*. Frontier Heritage Press, 1970.

15. Pratt, Richard Henry and Utley, Robert, M, ed. *Battlefield and Classroom: Four Decades with American Indians* (1867–1904). Lincoln, NE: University of Nebraska Press, 1987.

16. Secoy, Frank. *Changing Military Patterns on the Great Plains*. Monograph of the American Ethnological Society, No. 21. J.J. Augustine, Locust Valley, NY, 1953.

17. Riddle, Jefferson C. *Indian History of the Modoc War* (reprint of a 1914 publication). Saratoga, CA: Urion Press, 1974.

18. Ferguson, R. Brian and Whitehead, Neil L., eds. *War in the Tribal Zone: Expanding States and Indigenous Warfare*. Santa Fe, NM: Santa Fe School of American Research Press, 1992.

Indian Scouts

1. Warfield, Colonel H.B. *With Scout and Cavalry at Fort Apache*. Tucson, AZ: Arizona Pioneers Historical Society, 1965.

2. Downey, Fairfax and Jacobsen, Jacque Noel, Jr. *The Red/Bluecoats: The Indian Scouts, U.S. Army*. Fort Collins, CO: Old Army Press, 1973.

3. Danker, Donald F. "The North Brothers and the Pawnee Scouts," *Nebraska History* 42, Sept. 1961: pp. 161–179.

4. Innis, Ben. *Bloody Knife: Custer's Favorite Scout*. Fort Collins, CO: Old Army Press, 1973.

5. Mason, Dr. Joyce Evelyn. *The Use of Indian Scouts in the Apache Wars, 1870–1886*. Dissertation. Bloomington, IN: Indiana University, 1970.

6. Smith, Sherry L. *The View from Officers' Row, Army Perceptions of Western Indians*. Tucson, AZ: Univ. of Arizona Press, 1990.

7. Swett, Morris. "Seargent I-See-O, Kiowa Indian Scout," Oklahoma City, OK: *Chronicles of Oklahoma* 13, Sept. 1935: pp. 341–354.

8. Hollis, Marjor General Robert P. "The Army's Legendary Sgt. I-See-O," *Army* 27(6). Washington DC: June, 1977: pp 41–45.,

9. Dunlay, Thomas W. *Wolves for the Blue Soldiers: Indian Scouts and Auxiliaries with the US Army 1860–1890*. Lincoln, NE: Univ. of Nebraska Press, 1982.

Spanish American War (1898)

1. Roosevelt, Theodore. *The Rough Riders*. NY: Charles Scribner and Sons, 1899.

Mexican Border War (1916)

1. U.S. Army Records at Ft. Huachuca, Arizona, 1867–1947 (Unpublished). Ft. Huachuca Museum.

World War I

1. Records of the American Expeditionary Forces (WWI), 1917–23, Record Group 120. National Archives, Washington DC, 1920.

2. "From Scout To Doughboy: The National Debate Over Integrating American Indians into the Military, 1891–1917," *Western Historical Quarterly* 17, No. 4. Logan, UT: Western History Assoc., October, 1986.

3. Wise, Jennings C. *The Red Man in the New World Drama*. Washington DC: W.F. Roberts Co., 1931.

4. Parker, Arthur C. "The American Indian in the World War," *Southern Workman*, February, 1918.

5. *New Mexico Historical Review* (Indians of New Mexico in WWI) A. I, page 426. B. II, pages 41–2. C. X, pages 79–83 and 313–5. D. XI, pages 18–25.

6. Hale, Dr. Duane. "Forgotten Heroes: American Indians in World War I," *Four Winds*. Austin, TX: Autumn, 1982.

7. Barsh, Russell. *American Indians in World War I*. Dissertation, Seattle, WA: University of Washington.

World War II

1. Bersnstein, Alison R. *American Indians and World War II*. Norman, OK: University of Oklahoma Press, 1991.

2. "Indians At Work" (1941–45), Published by The Civilian Conservation Corps, Indian Division, Dept. of Interior; Seven issues were devoted to Indians serving in WWII.

3. *Indians in the War*. Published by Dept. of the Interior, Office of Indian Affairs, Chicago, 1945.

4. Wolfert, Ira. *American Guerilla in the Philippines*. NY, NY: Simon and Schuster, 1945.

5. Medal of Honor Historical Society (list of Medal of Honor winners), 1012 S. Hammerschmidt, Lombard, Illinois.

6. Paul, Doris A. *Navajo Code Talkers*. Philadelphia, PA: Dorrance & Co., 1973.

7. Clark, Ida Clyde. *American Women and the World War*. NY, NY: D. Appleton and Co., 1918.

8. *New Mexico Magazine*. (Navajos and WWII):

   A. Kay, E. "Big Trouble Comes-We All Fight." Oct. '41: p.14

   B. Kirk, R. "Dedication For War." Mar. '42: p.7

   C. Higgins, H. "Navajo Warriors." Oct. '43: p.12

9. Neuberger, Richard L. "The American Indian Enlists," *Asia and the Americas* 42. Nov. 1942: pp. 628–31.

10. Sergeant, Elizabeth. "The Indian Goes to War," *New Republic* 107. Nov. 30, 1942: pp. 708–09.

11. Kawano, Kenji, photog. *Warriors: Navajo Code Talkers.* Flagstaff, AZ: Northland Publishing Co, 1990.

12. Holm, Tom. "Fighting A White Man's War: The Extent and Legacy of American Indian Participation in World War II," *Journal of Ethnic Studies*, 9:2. Tucson, AZ: University of Arizona.

Vietnam

1. Holm, Tom. "Indian Veterans of the Vietnam War: Restoring Harmony Through Tribal Ceremony," *Four Winds.* Austin, TX: Autumn, 1982.

Gulf War, Operation Iraqi Freedom and Modern Times

1. Various Tribal Newspapers.

2. *News From Indian Country*, various articles.

3. Combs, Beverly. "The American Indian Still Fights On For His Country," *The Times* (Magazine). Sept. 5, 1983.

4. *Stars And Stripes* (newspaper), various articles; P.O. Box 1803, Washington DC 20013. 202-829-3225. John Carroll, editor.

5. *Indian Country Today* newspaper, various articles.

Sources of Additional Information on Indians in the Military: Archives/Collections/Contacts

This list consists of the various agencies and individuals that were contacted in the course of doing research for this project and may be useful to others who are researching projects on this or related topics.

National Archives

1. General Research Reference Room, 203, (Books, guides, etc.)

2. Microfilm Reading Room, 400, (open until 9 p.m.). Almost everything in the archives has been published on microfilm, requires an "M" # and roll #; microfilm copy machines available.

3. Military Reference Branch

    A. Revolutionary War to 1917—Room 11w: Army enlistment records, muster rolls, Adjutant General's correspondence, etc.

    B. 20th Century: WWI, WWII, Korea—Room 11e

    C. Vietnam Records—National Records Center, Suitland, Maryland

4. Civilian Reference Branch—Room 13e: Records from: Dept. of Interior, BIA, CCC, Indian schools, Commissioner of Indian Affairs personal papers, etc.

5. Still Picture Branch, 18th floor, 202-501-5455

    A. Army Signal Corps Collection

    B. U.S. Marine Corps Collection

    C. Dept. of Navy Photo Collection

    D. Office of War Information

    E. BIA Collection

6. Motion Picture Branch, Room G-13, 202-501-5449

    Newsreel footage, U.S. Marine Corps, Dpt. of Navy, Army Signal Corps, Private Collections. Some available on videocassette for viewing, others on 16mm and 35mm film. Viewing equipment must be reserved in advance.

7. National Archives Publication Sales, Room G-9. Guides to the archives and collections.

Department of Defense

Dept. of Defense Still Media Records Center

Code SSRC, Washington DC 20374-1681

*Photos taken since 1973 are considered active.

Smithsonian, Various Buildings on the Mall

1. National Museum of Natural History, 10th @ Constitution

    A. American Indian Program, JoAllyn Archambault, Anthropologist

    B. Anthropological Archives: 250,000 records, manuscripts, and photos relating to American Indians. Includes the archives of NCAI and the National Tribal Chairman's Association.

    C. Human Studies Film Archives: International collection of films, including footage of American Indians. example: Dixon-Wanamaker Expedition to Crow Agency, 1908 and Sanderson's Northwest Indian Footage, c.1926–32.

2. National Museum of American History, 12th @ Constitution

    A. American Indian Program, Rayna Green, PhD

    B. Division of Armed Forces History, Don Kloster

3. National Air and Space Museum, 7th @ Independence

    Library; Air Force Photo Collection (1861–1954), includes: Army Air Service, Army Air Corps—150,000 negatives of aircraft, personnel, bases, etc.

4. National Museum of the American Indian, National Mall;

    A. Rick West's Office, Andrea Hanley

    B. Public Affairs Office

Library of Congress

1. North American Indian Reference Librarian: Patrick Frazier, Jefferson Bldg.

2. Prints and Photo Collection, Madison Bldg., 3rd floor

   718 entries for Indian graphic material: Indians in their natural habitat, Civil War, Dixon-Wanamaker Expeditions, Individual portraits of warriors in regalia, scouts, etc.

3. Computer Catalog Center, Jefferson Bldg. (ties in to major collections, including photos; printouts available.)

Other Sources for Military Photos & Info in Washington DC

1. Center for Military History, HQDA

   Historical Properties Branch

   Attn: DAMH-HSO

   Washington DC 20314

   *This center has the Army War Art collection and all U.S. Army Museum collections.

2. Center For Military History, HQDA

   Organizational History Branch (Army unit histories)

   Attn: DAMH-HSO

   Washington DC 20314

3. Marine Corps Historical Center

   Washington Navy Yard

   Washington DC 20374-0580

4. Office of Public Affairs (Media and Authors)

   Dept. of Defense

   Room 2E765, The Pentagon

   Washington DC 20001

5. U.S. Naval Historical Center 202-433-2765

   Curator's Branch

Bldg. 108, Washington Navy Yard

Washington DC 20374

National Museum of the American Indian (New York City Location)

1. Indian Film & Video Collection; Elizabeth Weatherford/Millie Seubert
2. Photo Collection; Karen Firth/Lee Calendar
3. Research Branch, Bronx; American Indian Warfare

U.S. Army Military History Institute

Carlisle Barracks, PA 17013

Dr. Richard Summers, Archivist

*Civil War collection and other historical eras

U.S. Naval Institute Library

Preble Hall; Annapolis, MD 21402

*Collection of paintings, prints and photographs

Mathers Museum

603 East 8th; Bloomington, Indiana 47405

*8,000 images, Joseph K. Dixon photographer. Early 1900s, WWI, Indians

Bettman Archive, Inc.

136 East 57th St.; NY, NY 10022

*4 million items: History of Civilization, WWI, WWII (source for a few photos in the book *American Indians in World War II*).